UNDERGRADUATE FIELD INSTRUCTION PROGRAMS: CURRENT ISSUES AND PREDICTIONS

Edited by: Kristen Wenzel

COUNCIL ON SOCIAL WORK EDUCATION
345 East 46th Street   New York, N. Y. 10017

PREFACE

Undergraduate Field Instruction Programs: Current Issues and Predictions and its companion volume, Curriculum Guides For Undergraduate Field Instruction Programs, are published at a time when there is increasing recognition of the importance of field instruction in undergraduate social work programs.

The articles in this volume deal with issues facing educators involved in field instruction programs today. The issues concern: (1) the advantages and disadvantages of education for professional practice, (2) the pros and cons of using a curriculum in undergraduate field instruction programs, (3) the functions and dysfunctions of university-agency collaboration in providing quality field instruction, (4) the costs and benefits of undergraduate field instruction programs accruing to manpower development, and (5) the current status of undergraduate social work programs in general. These articles were written in connection with a workshop held for educators who had been participants in a two and a half year project on undergraduate field instruction.

The Council extends its sincere appreciation to the Veterans Administration whose grant made possible this project and the two attendant publications. It is a pleasure to give special recognition to Miss Claire R. Lustman, Chief, Staff Development and Education Division, Social Work Service, Veterans Administration, whose efforts contributed substantially to the initiation and development of this project; to Delwin M. Anderson, Director, Social Work Service, Veterans Administration, without whose constant support this project could not have been maintained; and to officials of the Education Service of the Department of Medicine and Surgery, Veterans Administration, whose early recognition of the importance of this project to the Veterans Administration's mission as an educational institution served as a constant source of encouragement to all participants.

Although the material contained in this volume is primarily oriented to undergraduate social work education, it is our hope that it will also serve the interests of graduate school educators.

Lilian Ripple
Acting Executive Director

September, 1971

iii

FOREWORD

Is field instruction in preparation for professional practice appropriate and consonant with the goals of a liberal arts education as well as with students' interests and needs today? Is the use of a curriculum in field instruction effective or artificial in promoting the socialization of students to the social work profession? Does quality social work education--and more specifically field instruction--require close collaboration between university and agency or is this an invalid and impractical assumption? To what extent do baccalaureate students with a background in social work content courses and skill development perform or not perform consistently more effectively than those students without such a background? These are the major questions to which the authors of the papers presented in this volume address themselves.

These questions arose and were identified as key issues in social work education at the baccalaureate level by university and agency faculty who participated in a two and a half year project known as the Undergraduate Field Experience Demonstration Project. The project was sponsored by the Veterans Administration and conducted under the leadership of the Council on Social Work Education. The primary goal of the project was to develop curriculum guides which would contain practical and illustrative material for use by field and university faculty throughout the country within their respective undergraduate social work programs to develop their own field instruction models. The project began in the Spring of 1969.

In order to achieve this goal, four demonstration units were set up in different sections of the country and were given two years with adequate resources to develop the type of field instruction program that would demonstrate the kind of learning that occurs in the field and the type of integration that develops between this and what is taught in the classroom. In addition to a well developed field instruction program each unit was expected to prepare a detailed curriculum guide for publication, taking into account the uniqueness of its respective academic, practice, and social settings. Four Veterans Administration installations and neighboring universities were selected to participate in the project. Each demonstration unit consisted of a university faculty member whose students were placed at the near-by Veterans Administration installation for field instruction, a field instructor appointed from among the professional social workers on the staff of the participating Veterans Administration installation and an educational consultant with expertise in curriculum development. The editor of this volume served as director of the project.

During the first eighteen months that this project was in operation, a number of issues regarding field instruction at the undergraduate level but not specifically related to curriculum development arose and had direct bearing on the project. Although the project was not designed to study those issues in depth, nevertheless, it was generally agreed to by the participants that a further examination of these issues would enhance the contribution this project could make to social work education. Consequently, towards the end of the second year of the project a workshop was planned providing just such an opportunity. The workshop was held in New Orleans from April 28-30, 1971, for the university and agency faculty participants as well as for the curriculum specialists who had served as consultants to social service departments where the students had done their field instruction were invited to attend the workshop. Miss Claire R. Lustman, the Veterans Administration representative from Central Office largely responsible for the funding of this project which included this workshop, was also in attendance.

Four key issues related to undergraduate field instruction were identified by the director and the coordinator of the project in consultation with the participants. Four outside experts, each familiar with one of these issues, were asked to attend and to serve both as resource people and as discussion leaders for one workshop session respectively. Each was asked to give about a twenty minute presentation and then to lead a discussion for approximately an hour and a half on what was presented. On the basis of their presentation and subsequent discussion with the rest of the participants, each was asked to write a paper, all of which appear in this volume.

The rationale on which the project was developed; that is, educationally focused field instruction through the use of a curriculum is the issue dealt with in the first paper. In an honest treatment of the pros as well as the cons of using a curriculum in undergraduate field instruction, Serapio Zalba exposes the abuses to which curriculum use has been subjected while at the same time making its continued use attractive and convincingly worthwhile even to those who have been alienated to such because of its negative impact.

A similar pro-con approach is taken by Kay Dea in his discussion of the functions and dysfunctions of the collaborative process for universities and agencies in providing quality social work education. He exposes the reader to a variety of types of patterns of collaboration with its attendant problems and then identifies what he calls a newly emerging pattern. His clear-cut and practical treatment of this latter pattern together with his creative handling of anticipated problems will enable field instructors to weigh more seriously the advantages and disadvantages of university-agency collaboration in their own respective programs.

Treating the subject of field instruction from yet another perspective, namely, from the viewpoint of the goals of the overall undergraduate social work program, Bernece Simon argues for a more liberal view of field instruction today. Drawing largely from her own experiences, she shows why this is absolutely necessary if we are to avoid the pitfall of the seeming irreconcilability between field instruction as education for practice and field instruction as liberal arts education.

There is no doubt that field instruction is a costly form of education for the university as well as for the agency. William Hill in his discussion of the impact of undergraduate field instruction programs on manpower development attempts to handle this difficult subject by giving to the reader and especially to the employer of baccalaureate level social workers, a broader insight into how to define and weigh the costs as well as the benefits accruing to an agency that makes its resources available to such programs.

These papers form the second part of this volume. In addition the Chairman of the CSWE Special Committee on Undergraduate Education, John A. Schiller, was asked to give an overview of undergraduate social work education at the opening session. His remarks are the subject of the first paper which serves as the introduction to this volume. Presented in a detailed and thorough manner they give to the reader an accurate and up-to-date analysis of the current status of undergraduate social work education.

Although the views of the university and agency faculty who participated in the project are reflected in a general way in the papers, their opinions on these same issues are presented more succinctly in the third part of this volume. Since the project participants dealt directly and intensely with these issues over a two-year period, it seems that including what they have to say in this form will enhance the value of this volume.

Recent developments in field instruction at the baccalaureate level are a catalytic force for the re-evaluation of the entire social work education continuum taking place in this decade of the 70's. This reality is strongly attested to by the papers presented in this volume.

I am indebted to Frank M. Loewenberg and Alfred Stamm for their assistance.

Kristen Wenzel

vii

TABLE OF CONTENTS

PART I: INTRODUCTION

THE CURRENT STATUS OF UNDERGRADUATE SOCIAL WORK EDUCATION

by

John A. Schiller*

Tremendous changes have occurred since 1952 when one year graduate programs were abolished and undergraduate social work education was practically eliminated. 1/ Today baccalaureate social work education has gained official respectability. The Undergraduate Field Experience Demonstration Project (funded by the Veterans Administration and directed by the Council on Social Work Education) is clear evidence of this change. The project represents a planned effort to develop a more educationally focused field instruction program in undergraduate social work education. Thus the "sine qua non" of social work education has been legitimized at the baccalaureate level.

During the two years this project was carried out, five other important actions were taken.

(1) By action of the National Association of Social Workers, graduates from undergraduate social work programs approved by the Council on Social Work Education became eligible for regular membership in the professional organization.

(2) The Council on Social Work Education established standards for approval of undergraduate social work programs that prepare for social work practice.

(3) New guidelines were developed to assure sounder practice oriented education in undergraduate programs.

(4) Recognition was given by the Board of Directors of CSWE to use "social work education" instead of "social welfare education" in designating undergraduate programs.

(5) Graduate schools were given more freedom to develop ways of granting advanced standing of up to one year to any group of students who have completed programs in an accredited college or university which in the opinion of its faculty is substantially equivalent to the academic content offered by the graduate school.

1/
Arnulf M. Pins, An Overview of Undergraduate Education in Social Welfare: Past Issues, Current Developments and Future Potentials (New York: Council on Social Work Education, 1968), P. 6.

---

*John Schiller is Chairman, Division of Social Sciences, Pacific Lutheran University, Tacoma, Washington, and Chairman of CSWE's Special Committee on Undergraduate Education.

Only by taking a quick look backward is it possible to appreciate the new status of baccalaureate social work education or the dynamics involved in its development.

The Curriculum Study Guide of 1959 revived "the dormant but not defunct controversy over graduate versus undergraduate social work education (or a combination thereof)." 2/ Its recommendations of a continuum of undergraduate-graduate education for social work and initiation of undergraduate social work education were rejected. Yet, two years later the first consultant in undergraduate social welfare education was employed by the Council. However, the first CSWE guidelines prepared for undergraduate programs appeared to encourage only the development of social welfare content, emphasizing "learning about" rather than "learning to do." 3/

Minutes of the Special Committee on Undergraduate Education provide an interesting commentary on the dynamics of movement from social welfare content in undergraduate education to undergraduate social work education. 4/ It is to be noted that the use of the words "social work" instead of "social welfare" is indicative of the nature of the argument as well as of the change that has occurred. Again and again the committee struggled with the question of moving undergraduate programs to a social work education model.

As manpower needs of the nation demanded a larger number of skilled persons in its social service delivery system and as leaders in professional social work education re-evaluated their programs, opinions shifted. In 1965 the Board of Directors of CSWE decided to extend the range of the Council's concerns more rigorously, both in principle and practice, beyond its core responsibility for the advancement of professional education to the broader scope of training and

---

2/

Katherine A. Kendall, "Issues and Problems in Social Work Education" Social Work Education Reporter, Vol. 14, No. 1 (March, 1966), P. 37.

3/

Katharine N. Handley, Mereb E. Mossman, and Lucille K. Barber, Three Articles on Social Welfare Content in Undergraduate Education (New York: Council on Social Work Education, 1962).

4/

This Committee was established in an advisory capacity to the Board of Directors and to the Council staff: (1) in developing the undergraduate project; (2) in encouraging sound development of undergraduate social welfare programs; (3) in identifying, with the Curriculum Committee, the curriculum objectives, content and organization in undergraduate social welfare education; and (4) in studying the relationship of this education to professional education for social work and to social work practice in positions not now requiring professional education.

education to meet all social work manpower needs. During the next two years the Special Committee on Undergraduate Education developed a new set of guidelines and envisioned undergraduate programs preparing students for graduate professional education and for employment in social welfare. Though the 1967 Guide recommended field experience as desirable it was not required. Though a sequence of courses in social welfare was suggested, faculty with expertise in social work were not required. Though preparation for employment in the field of social welfare was one of four possible goals for the undergraduate program, programs could become constituent members of CSWE without having such a goal. 5/ Programs were not yet practice oriented.

Beginning with 1963, the Council on Social Work Education sponsored institutes and workshops and contracted for special assignments to develop materials for undergraduate courses and programs. Here a progression to the present state of preparation for practice is also demonstrated. The first series of workshops were concerned with "learning about" rather than "learning to do" social work. The first several workshops resulted in several syllabi to develop a course on Social Welfare as a Social Institution. 6/ Two years later content dealing with social work as a profession in the field of social welfare was prepared. 7/ In 1967 supportive material for the field experience part of undergraduate education was provided. 8/ But the criteria were not specific enough to require that every program include field experience in its series of courses. Nor was the sentiment such that learning to do social work at beginning practice levels was seen as the goal of field experience. Not until 1971 did the Council develop course content around "learning to do" social work. 9/ The title of the publication made clear the stage of development in undergraduate social work education: The Teaching of Practice Skills in Undergraduate Programs in Social Welfare and Other Helping Services. Had the publication come out three months later it might have been entitled, "...in Social Work and Other Helping Services."

5/

Undergraduate Programs in Social Welfare: A Guide to Objectives, Content, Field Experience and Organization (New York: Council on Social Work Education, 1967).

6/

Herbert Bisno, Richard H. P. Mendes, Irving Piliavin, and John Romanyshyn, Social Welfare as a Social Institution (New York: Council on Social Workk Education, 1963).

7/

Irving B. Tebor and Patricia B. Pickford, Social Work, A Helping Profession in Social Welfare (New York: Council on Social Work Education, 1966).

8/

Margaret B. Matson, Field Experience in Undergraduate Programs in Social Welfare (New York: Council on Social Work Education, 1967).

9/

Frank M. Loewenberg and Ralph Dolgoff, Teaching Practice Skills in Undergraduate Programs in Social Welfare and Other Helping Services (New York: Council on Social Work Education, 1971).

In the meantime junior colleges were developing programs for new careerists and community workers. Indigenous people active in Headstart, Office of Economic Opportunity programs, and other federally funded programs were also seeking educational help in preparing themselves more effectively as workers in human services. Undergraduate staff of the Council sought out the junior colleges and were invited to help develop associate of arts degree programs. By 1969 the guidelines for Associate Arts Community Service Degrees had been developed. 10/ The impact of such programs are just beginning to be felt by baccalaureate degree social work education.

PROGRAMS TODAY

Specific requirements were developed by the Special Committee on Undergraduate Education, submitted through the Commission on Educational Services to the Board of Directors, and approved by the Board of Directors of the Council in April, 1970. 11/ Since the Fall of 1970, educational institutions wanting approval of their undergraduate social work programs, need to develop a program that clearly has the goal of preparing persons for practice in social work. The Board also established the Committee on Standards for Undergraduate Social Work Programs. This committee of eleven members is charged to develop criteria operationalizing the standards. The undergraduate functions of the Council now tend to parallel the graduate functions of the Council. At each level one committee concerns itself with program content and at each level another committee concerns itself with program approval. One distinction must be noted, however: at the undergraduate level programs are approved; at the graduate level accreditation is given to graduate schools of social work.

And now, let's take a closer look at the nature of those programs in undergraduate social work education that follow the 1971 Standards for Approval of Undergraduate Social Work Programs. We will examine their characteristics by comparing the present standards to past criteria. This will clarify the present nature of undergraduate social work education.

10/

The Community Service Technician: Guide for Associate Degree Programs in The Community and Social Services (New York: Council on Social Work Education, 1970).

11/

New Requirements for Undergraduate Programs in Social Welfare Seeking Constituent Membership in the Council on Social Work Education (New York: Council on Social Work Education, 1970).

COMPARISON OF CRITERIA FOR UNDERGRADUATE PROGRAMS IN SOCIAL WORK EDUCATION
TO 1967 AND 1961 GUIDELINES*

1971	1967	1961
1. It is accredited by its regional accrediting association to award a baccalaureate degree.	Same	Same
2. It identifies and describes the undergraduate program in social work in its catalogue.	Same	Not required
3. It requires a coherent educational program including:		
a. a broad liberal arts base.	Recommended but not required	Recommended but not required
b. courses with social work content.	A sequence of courses to meet stated objectives	Not required
c. appropriate educationally directed field instruction with direct engagement in service activities designed to meet the stated educational objectives.	Provides opportunity for field experience	Provides opportunity for observation
4. It submits a written statement of the educational objectives of the program.	Same	Not required
5. It indicates on the transcript, diploma or other permanent record, that the student has successfully completed the program in social work.	Not required	Not required
6. It assigns to the program a full-time faculty member qualified to provide leadership for, and assume administration of, the undergraduate social work program.	Same	Not required
7. It shows faculty resources adequate in terms of experience, training and number to carry out the objectives of the program, including full-time faculty with a graduate degree from an accredited school of social work.	Not required	Not required

	1971	1967	1961
8. It assigns faculty with a graduate degree from an accredited school of social work to teach the content on social work practice.		Not required	Not required
9. It consents to, and collaborates, in a site visit in the process of determining approval of the program.		Not required	Not required
10. It reaffirms annually that the program continues to meet all standards.		Not required	Not required
11. It operates its program without discrimination in regard to race, color, creed, national origin, age, and sex.		Not required	Not required

* Source: Standards for Approval of Undergraduate Programs in Social Work

Programs must have a well developed set of goals. And the means of achieving these goals need to be spelled out very clearly. No longer is it enough to list a goal and several courses. There must be a cohesive planned educational objective. This must be supported with a precisely described educational plan and program that will achieve the educational objective. And for program approval the goal is to prepare for practice in social work. In other words, a sound educational program is required that will prepare undergraduates to begin to do social work with some level of autonomy. Furthermore, an institution must do more than develop this program on paper. Site visits will be made to every school to assess objectively the correctness of the description of the program. Employers of graduates from approved programs will have assurance that the educational program of colleges meeting CSWE standards for approval means something.

The student will have supportive documentation that he has completed an approved program in undergraduate social work education. Some kind of certification upon graduation will be given to the student. Some schools indicate this on the transcript and/or provide a special certificate that a student has completed the social work program. Some schools offer a Bachelor of Arts degree with a major in social work. Though now social work programs appear most often under the aegis of the Department of Sociology in the College of Arts and Sciences, an increasing number of schools are offering a social work major in its own right. A growing number of schools are giving a Bachelor's Degree in Social Work or Social Welfare. Though their number is still small, it may not be long before the majority of programs will provide their graduates with a B.S.W. degree.

There is still debate about the most desirable way of structuring an educational program that will maintain the liberal arts context while developing a major or program that is professional. It seems wise, however, to retain the liberal arts context. For we are convinced that social work education attains its richest development when built upon a sound liberal arts foundation. Constant sharing between liberal arts disciplines and social work education assures providing social work education with the conceptual tools and processes necessary to develop the theoretical and skills components of social work practice. Furthermore, a close relationship between social work education and liberal arts education will facilitate and maximize the contributions that social work education ought properly make to liberal arts education.

More than ever, the Council on Social Work Education is aware of the need to develop a sound sequence of courses in both the foundation disciplines and in the social work sequence. But conclusions about the most desirable sequence in both areas are still waiting to be reached. During May 1971 the first workshop to develop models of undergraduate programs

9

was sponsored by the Council. The greatest challenge for colleges that desire to have their programs approved by the Council is to develop sound undergraduate programs. Nor should such efforts simply take graduate models and introduce them at the undergraduate level. It is my contention that undergraduate social work education can be more flexible and innovative and thus meet the changing demands of society upon the social work profession more effectively. Now is the time to build from the "bottom up" as Herbert Bisno argued. 12/

Research about the process of socialization into a profession sheds some light on this factor. Thus far most of the research that has been done on the socialization process into the profession about graduate and undergraduate professional education seems to reach the same conclusion. Professional education is conducted in such a fashion that students graduate with a professional self-concept that has molded them in such a way that the profession finds it difficult to innovate and meet the changing challenges of the service needs and kind of problems that the profession ought to be resolving or meeting. In this the social work profession is no exception. This does not mean that the social work profession is oblivious to the problem. But, as is true of any institutionalized process it is slow to change. In fact, having become perpetuators of a certain viewpoint with a high degree of commitment prevents ease of innovation and change of values and their concomitant behaviors.

The challenge to undergraduate social work education is to carry out two goals. One goal is to help students acquire those values that are the strengths of social work practice. The second goal is to preserve that fresh free approach to individual and societal problem solving that is required for a dynamic pluralistic community developing around us. Undergraduate liberal education ought to be the setting most amenable to such an educational adventure. This demands that one not import "in toto" what has been the process or structure in graduate social work education.

FOUNDATION AND SUPPORTIVE COURSES

Some general recommendations can be offered. Students need exposure to all of the social sciences if they are going to be able to adequately analyze strategies of intervention. For example, poverty has its economic, historical, political, psychological, and sociological dimensions. And whether one works with a single client or is concerned with changing the societal or community setting in which the client experiences his problem, none of these dimensions of analysis in problem solving can be avoided.

12/
    Herbert Bisno, "A Theoretical Framework for Teaching Social Work Methods and Skills, with Particular Reference to Undergraduate Social Welfare Education" Journal of Education for Social Work, Vol. 5, No. 2 (Fall, 1969) pp. 5-17.

Furthermore, advocacy functions and organizing groups in the population
for self-help action programs require a broader knowledge base. If you
examine some of the conceptual tools Bisno has suggested in his article
on theory and concepts underlying the teaching of methods and skills to
undergraduates, you will discover that these functions describing social
work practice demand the use of concepts and processes developed and explicated in business, economics, political science, psychology and
sociology. 13/

Courses in social welfare systems or institutions, in social work
practice, micro or macro in nature, and in field instruction require
such academic resources if the student is going to excel in learning to
work as a social worker today.

In this respect undergraduate program development has different
opportunities than has been true of graduate social work. Up until now
graduate schools have not specified content pre-requisites for admission.
Thus, graduate courses needed to provide broad social science knowledge
that sensitized the social worker in analytic abilities. Undergraduate
education in social work has challenging opportunities to individualize
and maximize the social science analytic competencies of its graduates.
Proper course area requirements in the undergraduate program will enable
students to approach social work curriculum with appropriate underpinnings
of theory and concepts taught by personnel with expertise in their own
disciplines.

This is especially true of those students who already know in which
kinds of settings he plans to work. For them it becomes possible to
become more selective in the foundation courses as well as in the courses
pursued in related fields while taking the social work courses. This will
maximize the student's in-depth understanding of those supportive disciplines as related to his social work curriculum. For example, one-to-one
helping relationships would argue for greater competency in psychology.
Social intervention at the macro level of social behavior would call for
greater exposure to economics, political science and sociology. A note
of warning should be given at this point. Undergraduate programs that
are too prescriptive do not provide the flexibility of meeting individual
student needs. In other words, sound planning would permit structuring
a program that maximizes supportive content but that provides appropriate
flexibility. The rationale for the present movement in higher education
to provide students with a bachelor's degree that does not have a specific
major but frees the student to develop his own academic program in a
general studies kind of degree seems appropriate for adaptation to educational planning in undergraduate social work education.

13/
   Ibid.

11

Another aspect of planning the foundation disciplines component concerns the faculty and specific courses. Some larger universities may ' choose to hire special faculty to teach courses, they may create courses in an effort to provide the kind of content felt necessary for social workers. In both of these approaches the goal too often is to hire social workers to teach these courses. But this has hazards. Social workers cannot be specialists in all disciplines. And the challenges of non-social work viewpoints are lost. Diversity of faculty from other disciplines who are experts in their own field is one of the best ways to prevent the undesirable aspects of professional socialization and to force the social work faculty to sell the social work approach within the dialogue of alternative viewpoints. This is true liberal education.

Some schools may use the easy way out by selecting courses from the foundation disciplines that, on the basis of course title and description, seem to have desirable content. But this is not sound education. Rather, planning sessions with faculty from the foundation disciplines should be held. Here discussion between social workers and other specialists can occur. Social work educators must make clear the needs of social work students in terms that other disciplines can appreciate and to which they can respond. At the same time social work educators need to communicate the stance of social work toward problem solving. Other disciplines need to communicate their perspective and contribution to social work education. Through such interdisciplinary discussion more appropriate course content can be developed and intelligent choices of courses can be made from those disciplines as a student's program is created.

Past efforts at interdisciplinary courses have not been very successful. There are indications that traditional discipline boundaries are crumbling; that new courses being developed will repackage knowledge about man and his environment. Thus it seems necessary to foster a sharing of the contributions and concerns of the various purveyors of knowledge in the educational system so that students are provided with the appropriate academic tools to function in the community at their chosen location.

Communication between faculty of various fields will lead to another sharing pattern. When each properly understands the other's contribution to a particular issue each faculty member is free to participate in the other person's particular course for that lecture or lectures in which each has his own expertise and perspective. For example, as social workers and economists share their perspectives and knowledge about poverty and the economic system or economic theory, they can help one another to broaden the input and thus enhance the students' understanding of economics and of social work.

The social worker can be invited to present his perspective and understanding to an economics class and the economist can be invited to present his expertise to a class in social intervention at the macro as well as the micro levels. The educational experience of both faculty and students will be strengthened. Provincial education will be overcome.

Social work practice concerns itself with values. This is true both for the social worker in his practice and for the clients and for the social arrangements of society in which the client lives. Just to assume that the values espoused by the profession and to which the student is espoused in social work courses is enough will not suffice. Students must be confronted with an analysis of values and value systems as presented by other disciplines. Courses in the humanities provide such an opportunity. Here again the social work faculty needs dialogue with humanities faculty to experience the crucible of debating values and problem solving. A cloistered development of a professional value orientation is not healthy.

It is appropriate to note here that this is exactly the same kind of argument presented by minority spokesmen when they argue for the inclusion of minority life styles and value systems in social work education. Too often social workers have discovered they were imposing solutions or interpretations upon problems from a middle class perspective. So, too, value systems of a profession grow out of a restricted perspective. The sociology of knowledge should alert us to such facts. More recently phenomenology in sociology has shown that values and perspectives about life are formed in like fashion. Because of our life history or our professional background we assume that our value system is right or valid.

Of equal importance is the effect that social work faculty can have upon faculty from other disciplines. Up until recently the contributions that social workers have made to liberal arts education has been minimal. This is due primarily to the isolation at the graduate level. Undergraduate social work education has the chance to change this situation. This is one of the strongest arguments for keeping it in the liberal arts structure of the university. Now that the program has been strengthened and legitimized social work education can make its own contribution to liberal arts education directly and indirectly. In fact, this is one of its greatest challenges. It can be trite to express it so but social work can put "heart" into undergraduate liberal arts education. For social work values cannot be left out of the educational process. They are as applicable to the educational process as they are to family counseling or to working with clients in a correctional setting. Teaching methods, student-faculty relationships, course goals and faculty responsibility for the student's academic success as well as his success as a person in a college community are going to be affected by the stance of the social work educator.

A working principle in curriculum development has been that we are really talking about a variety of curricula as long as the primary goal of preparation for practice is realized. The particular curriculum developed (1) must be based on a sound rationale, (2) its content must be designed to achieve the goals established, and (3) it must take into account contemporary developments in higher education.

For the moment we will by-pass two other issues undergraduate programs must consider, the relationship of the baccalaureate program to associate of arts degree programs and to graduate programs. We will, then, first take a closer look at the baccalaureate social work program.

Evidence seems to indicate that college students need an early exposure to the functions carried out by social workers and the settings in which they work. Self-identification with the specific career of social work is either lacking or has been negative for many college students. Several methods can be used to achieve this goal: (1) offer a freshman-sophomore introductory course in the field of social work; (2) have social workers teach courses like social problems or man in society in which students experience the social work perspective in the analysis of human behavior and problem solving; (3) have social workers teach units in courses offered by the various departments of the social sciences; or (4) develop a team-teaching model for certain courses in the social sciences or humanities.

At the same time students need an early exposure to the community in which they experience social behavior as an analytic or problem solving challenge. Such opportunities can be provided in the social work curriculum through field observation, field experience, and field instruction. Though one usually thinks of these three levels of involvement as sequential, reaching the field instruction level in the senior year, it needs to be recognized that all three levels may be experienced in varying degrees at all levels of a student's college career. Degrees of autonomy and intensity or complexity in such experiences will vary with each student and with the nature of the experience.

The philosophy of higher education today has moved to an integration of the classroom and the community, mediating the university learning experience with the community in which the present life and future destiny of America is being forged. The acquisition of knowledge and the use of knowledge has been merged in liberal education. It would be ironic to find sociology students, political science students and psychology students having more analytic and service delivery experience than social work students. Such could be the case if social work educators do not keep abreast of what is happening in liberal arts education and in other undergradudate professional education.

It is necessary for the social work curriculum to provide an historical perspective to the process of meeting human needs and the complex nature of the structures and functions by which human services are performed, a meaningful understanding of the philosophy and place of social work in the delivery of human services, and an adequate understanding of and experience in the functions carried out by social workers.

Undergraduate courses in the history and contemporary structures of social service delivery systems have moved beyond the traditional introductory social welfare course. Just this year two publications are appearing, one by Herbert Bisno and the other by John Romanyshyn, that are giving a different and more meaningful approach to such course content. 14/ Previous conceptualizations, range of interrelationships and processes of development of the institutionalization of meeting human needs have been too narrowly professional and parochial. Such courses need to organize information around various models of cultural and institutional development, for example, the evolutionary model, the equilibrium model, the conflict model. A holistic analysis must be included so that special courses, for example, child welfare legislation, do not distort a student's analytic and problem solving approaches.

Social work methods and interventive skills have moved to a much broader focus. Traditional concepts and tools are being questioned and reviewed. Non-traditional approaches are being validated. Here again, undergraduate social work education has a unique opportunity.

Social work practice has not been described very well when using the traditional terms casework, group work and community organization. What has been described in the past by use of these terms are the settings in contrast to methods in which social workers often functioned in carrying out social work practice; namely, one-to-one relationships, working with groups, and with the larger community. As new possible settings for social work practice develop, these traditional terms make it difficult to provide potential students and the supporting public with an adequate picture of what social workers really do and where the opportunities for social work positions actually are.

Undergraduate social work education has a great opportunity to build a new conceptual framework for social work practice. One approach has been to describe social work practice in generalist terms. Such terminology is supported with several distinct arguments which are not necessarily supportive of each other; (1) skills taught at the undergraduate level are generic in nature and at a less complex and less specialized level so that they are transferable to any helping situation, (2) undergraduate education is not technical and therefore does not prepare graduates to perform in only one or in any specific setting, and (3) social work skills learned in any of the three traditional settings are transferable to any of the other settings.

14/

See Herbert Bisno, Social Work: Structure, Function and Change (New York: Harper & Row, forthcoming); and John Romanyshyn, Social Welfare: Charity to Justice (New York: Random House, 1971).

Another approach has been to categorize the behaviors social workers engage in as they perform their functions under new conceptual tools. Bisno has developed one such approach. He sees the social worker functioning in macro and micro transactional systems. Within those systems the techniques and skills of social work method fall into the following groupings: adversary, conciliatory, developmental, facilitative-instructional, knowledge development and testing, restorative, regulatory, rule-implementing and rule-making processes, techniques, and skills. 15/ Dolgoff has subsumed social work skills under the concepts of listening, interviewing, information-gathering, analysis and planning for intervention, engagement-interaction, intervention and implementation skills, referral processes, work setting skills, and self-evaluation. 16/

Undergraduate education is free from tradition in developing such conceptual models. Furthering this process demands educational expertise and innovation, the best scholarship in social work education. It points to the kinds of criteria that should be used in choosing undergraduate faculty. Undergraduate programs should be staffed with the most qualified social work educators available.

Most undergraduate programs will need to work hard at giving breadth to the social work practice component. Appropriating processes described by the various sciences of social behavior and translating them into interventive skills is the necessary but exacting task required if social workers are to be equipped with a fuller and more adequate range of techniques and skills. Interaction within the liberal arts setting will facilitate this task.

Related to this task is the setting in which undergraduates are provided field observation, field experience and field instruction. Classroom instruction and field learning are to be integrated. It has been customary to place students in settings providing social work field instruction. Certainly such a setting maximizes the opportunity of role-identification, self-awareness and learning skills. However, it does curtail the development of new settings in which non-traditional as well as traditional social work skills can be learned and in which social workers may then more often be employed.

Some schools have experimented with placements in legislative or other government offices, in business and industrial locations and in social advocacy opportunities unrelated to agency or institutional programs. This puts a much greater burden on the classroom instructor. It requires sharing the purposes and goals of field instruction with supervisory personnel not familiar with social work values and practices. Or if there is no supervisory staff, as may often be the case, it will require that the classroom instructor serve as a facilitator so that the student will be able to function in his field placement.

15/
  Bisno, ibid.

16/
  Loewenberg and Dolgoff, op. cit.

As more and more of the burden of field instruction falls upon the class-room instructor, student-faculty teaching ratios must be lowered. Since one of the primary goals of field instruction is to provide the student with an understanding of himself in the helping process, the abilities of the classroom instructor responsible for field instruction and of the field instructor becomes crucial. The experience of the Committee on Standards for Undergraduate Social Work Programs in evaluating effective field instruction will help determine appropriate criteria to assure quality field instruction. This becomes a necessity if the employing public is to be assured a qualified and competent baccalaureate level social worker.

Various models of field instruction are being used at the undergraduate level. Placement for two semesters of academic credit, during the regular academic year--anywhere from 8 to 16 hours per week--seems to be a promising expectation for field instruction. In some schools that have adopted the 4-1-4 calendar (four months of regular classes--one month in which the student has only one course--and another four months of regular courses) students have a field placement for the entire year and are then able to use the month in which only one course is taken as the time to spend four full weeks, eight hours a day, in the agency. Agencies and institutions find this most effective. Some schools use the summer as a follow-up of the regular school year for a continued and more extensive and intensive agency experience. It should be noted that anything less than 8 hours per week is highly inadequate if the goal is to develop skills for social work practice.

Thus far in our presentation it has been assumed that it is possible to educate for beginning practice at the undergraduate level and that enough is known about the nature and complexity of skills that can be taught to undergraduates. Is this really the case? The Undergraduate Field Experience Demonstration Project sponsored by the Council on Social Work Education and the Veterans Administration shows conclusively that this can be done. 17/ Each project was able to describe the behaviors learned and concepts taught that related to those behaviors. In every setting students were able to operate autonomously around various functions. More than 50 percent of the functions performed by master's degree social workers could be performed by undergraduates.

Support for this viewpoint is given by the social work manpower project at Syracuse University. The Manpower Task Force of the Syracuse University Undergraduate Curriculum Building Project developed a model of the performance expectations of the B.A. social worker. They were able to identify specific expectations that the B.A. social worker should be able to meet in his work. They summarized their findings thus:

17/

See the Companion Volume, Curriculum Guides for Undergraduate Field Instruction Programs (New York: Council on Social Work Education, 1972).

In general, the baccalaureate social worker will be utilized in gathering and ordering of knowledge on which a social diagnosis and treatment or action plan can be based. He will be utilized in establishing and maintaining a relationship of mutual trust necessary for effective interventive action and service provision. He will participate with other team members and the MSW team leader or consultant in identifying the nature of the problems presented and establishing the appropriate method and level of intervention and service provision. He will carry full responsibility for continuing service when the determined level of intervention is within his competence and may participate in service provision along with the MSW social worker in more complicated situations. He will be in regular communication with his team leader or consultant as new information or changing situations alter either the diagnosis or the preferred method of intervention, moving in and out of the situation as the focus of the particular episode of service changes.

These, then are the anticipated characteristics, qualities and behaviors which can be expected of the graduate of a curriculum in social work at the baccalaureate level. With experience, some may exceed these expecatations and their performance may be indeed indistinguishable from that of the worker with advanced education. 18/

Earlier we indicated that self-awareness as a social worker was a primary goal of field instruction. And it has also been established that such an experience is most appropriate during the senior year. This being the case, the educational process must have provided some screening process prior to the senior year. Otherwise a larger number of students than is desirable will discover that social work is not for them at a rather late period in their educational careers. It will certainly not be possible to develop a screening process that will guarantee that everyone will go through the senior year reaching the conclusion that social work is for him.

No effective solutions have been found that satisfactorily screen students during their first years in college. Early exposures to social work experiences, careful career counseling during the first two years of college by the social work faculty, and appropriate kinds of contacts with social work faculty in and out of the classroom and with senior social work students will help students screen themselves out of or into the program. A very crucial time is when students counsel with faculty in registering for upper division social work courses and when seeking field experience and field instruction placements. Limited student-faculty ratios are required to maximize student-faculty relationships for effective academic and career counseling. Because of the liberal arts setting, it is not feasible to refuse students admission to classes if they meet academic standards. And it must also be remembered that the ability to accurately assess whether a student has the necessary characteristics to succeed in social work practice is questionable. The problem hasn't even been solved with absolute certainty in graduate social work education.

_____

18/

Robert L. Baker, Thomas L. Briggs and Dorothy Bird Daly, Educating the Undergraduate for Professional Social Work Roles (Syracuse, N.Y.: Syracuse University Press, 1971), pp. 11.

It goes without saying that the demands of undergraduate programs in social work education require nothing less than a full-time faculty member to administer the program. And it becomes self-evident that it requires full-time social workers on the faculty with a minimum of a master's degree in social work from an accredited graduate school of social work.

In fact it has been our experience that it is highly impossible to develop and implement an effective undergraduate social work program with less than two social workers. Just the coordination of the field instruction program itself, for fifteen to thirty students demands half of one instructor's time.

Sufficient staffing will be one of the greatest hurdles for undergraduate social work. The very nature of the program will attract large numbers of students. At the very time that public and private higher education is finding it difficult to increase its manpower, student enrollments in social work courses are increasing rapidly. An additional dilemma is to find qualified undergraduate social work educators. Graduate schools have just recently begun to develop curricula that will provide social workers with teaching competencies. The Council on Social Work Education has sought support to sponsor two to four workshops every summer for the last few years to help new teachers and those social workers presently teaching to better equip themselves for the task.

In some instances graduate schools have either assumed or have been given the responsibility of developing and staffing undergraduate programs in their own universities. With present budgeting problems, universities are faced with momentous decisions. Shall the undergraduate program be developed at the expense of the graduate program? At the same time that such a problem presents itself, graduate schools are also feeling the pressure of the field to develop more doctoral programs in social work. But when all is said and done, the future should provide us with an enlarged number of more competent social workers at all levels of the educational spectrum.

STUDENT POPULATION

Another dimension of undergraduate education is the kind of students who are now coming to college. College students are more mature today than college students were five or ten years ago. A larger number of adults are returning to college either to finish their college degrees or to retool themselves to seek another career. Such a new career choice is often sought in the field of social work or other related human services. This is associated with the urge arising in adults to become part of the answer to the problems now confronting American society. A larger number of college transfer students will have had some social work courses and various kinds of field experiences in junior college programs. "New Careers" students having had diverse life experiences and experiences in some form of the helping services and who have had some junior college work, even as much as two full years, will be seeking admission to four year programs.

Minority students (racial, ethnic and low income) will be seeking admission into undergraduate social work programs. This will place additional demands upon the program and its instructors. It should be noted that one of the greatest needs in America today is to educate persons from minority groups so that those minority groups can be served by their own people and in addition so that the minorities can be included in the mainstream of American society. These concerns need to be met by the program and the university.

First, economic support must make it possible for minority students to have access to higher education and social work education. Secondly, a university that seeks to make it possible for minority students to come to a school must also provide the kinds of educational services that will enable these students to attain academic excellence. And, third, the skills and techniques that are provided in the curriculum should be appropriate to the kinds of services required.

As quality undergraduate social work programs are developed, these programs also need to address themselves to continuing education. The social services field employs many persons whose educational background was a non-social work B.A. degree. Some persons will have had less than a B.A. degree. In either instance, such persons are seeking to re-educate themselves and update their competencies as the needs of society change and as the structures and functions of social delivery systems change. Persons in the field who have non-social work B.A. degrees will need this kind of opportunity since the National Association of Social Workers has opened regular membership to such persons if they will gain the educational equivalencies to the kinds now offered by universities whose undergraduate social work programs are approved by CSWE. Undergraduate social work education must address itself to the educational needs of persons already in the field.

Several other new developments in higher education will be affecting undergraduate social work programs. More opportunities of receiving college credit through challenge exams, extension courses, "college with no walls" concepts, and televised classes are being provided. Educational institutions are giving academic credit for work experiences and/or life experiences. College level examination programs make it possible for students to get credit by examination for as much as one full year of foundation courses. One or two schools have developed a three-year baccalaureate degree program. Each of these opportunities has implications for the knowledge base with which students enter the social work program. It certainly presents the question of excusing students from a certain number of courses in the social work program.

THE CONTINUUM

As students who come from junior colleges have already completed social work courses and field experience as part of a community services technician program seek admission to baccalaureate programs, undergraduate schools are facing issues akin to those graduate schools must face when admitting students coming from quality baccalaureate social work programs.

Junior college social work programs include courses in interventive skills and field experience. 19/ This raises the question of the most desirable sequence in social work education. Should it move from the specific to the general or from the general to the specific? The question is complicated by the fact that junior college programs, at the present time, need not meet standards set by the social work profession. The fact remains, however, that students from such junior college programs will be seeking admission to baccalaureate programs in social work education.

Each institution will have the responsibility of assessing the knowledge base the student acquired and the adequacy of the field instruction provided. Such decisions ought to correspond, however, with the two-fold goal of providing quality social work education as well as considering the competencies and needs of the transferring student. Social work values and social work practice should prevent institutional rigidity from hurting the appropriate academic progress of the "client" who in this instance happens to be the student.

One guiding principle that may provide help is to think of the educational continuum in social work practice along the lines of complexity of theory and practice as well as autonomy in making decisions. With that frame of reference in mind, students coming from junior college programs can be given a program that builds upon previous education and experience. Another guideline to keep in mind when integrating junior college education with baccalaureate programs is that education at the junior college level is task oriented (technicians); whereas baccalaureate programs are oriented to the integration of concept and practice in terms of both the liberal arts support courses and the social work courses and oriented to learning that permits non-specific transfer of theory and skills. This distinction is most pronounced in field instruction during the senior year.

Undergraduate baccalaureate programs must also direct their concerns to the graduate schools of social work. This year's decision by the CSWE Board of Directors to permit graduate schools to provide advanced standing requires that colleges with undergraduate programs need to be in dialogue with graduate schools. 20/ Undergraduate schools will need to provide graduate schools with

---

19/

The Community Service Technician, op. cit.

20/

This is stated in the Manual of Accrediting Standards as follows:
A school may grant advanced standing of up to one year to any specified category of students who have completed a program in an accredited college or university which in the opinion of a school's faculty is substantially equivalent to the graduate school academic content missed by granting such advanced standing. (3613) (New York: Council on Social Work Education, 1971) p. 16.

appropriate curriculum information. Graduate schools need to be open to the changing nature of undergraduate social work education. Unless such open dialogue occurs in planning the continuum of social work education, students will again become victims of the rigidities of educational institutions and experience poor education. Undergraduate programs that qualify for program approval must do nothing less than provide quality education. Such programs may easily provide the student with the equivalent of the first year of graduate social work education now provided by many graduate schools. And if graduate schools do not want to "turn off" their first-year students coming from quality undergraduate programs they will have to provide advanced standing or a different kind of program for such students. Some such dialogue and program planning has already occurred.

At the present time undergraduate consultants and members of the undergraduate special committee of the Council on Social Work Education, as well as many undergraduate faculty, still receive too many complaints from students during their first year of graduate school. The complaint of non-challenging repetition runs the gamut of research methods courses, social work history and practice courses, and field instruction.

Present literature describing the goals of graduate education seems to indicate that the master's degree social workers will now be functioning as supervisors, consultants, administrators, planners, teachers, trainers, researchers, developers, and specialized services. This seems to justify the efforts of undergraduate education to prepare B.A. social workers to perform many of the direct services demanded by clients, groups, agencies, institutions, communities, and society with the ability to perform autonomously at certain levels.

RELATIONSHIPS WITH THE FIELD

Faculty of undergraduate programs will need to develop appropriate relationships with staff and agencies and institutions in which their students will be placed for field instruction. They must also be in constant consultation with potential employers of B.A. social workers.

One of the recurring complaints at the recent hearings on the length of graduate social work education was that master's graduates were not prepared to provide direct services in the agency or institution. It was also apparent that agency persons were not in touch with the kinds of educational programs now existing in graduate schools of social work. What clues does this provide for undergraduate programs?

Several suggestions seem appropriate. (1) There must be a close work-ing relationship between field instructor and classroom instructor in the development of curriculum content and the teaching of curriculum content. (2) Field instructors should be given the kind of faculty status that pro-vides them with an avenue of affecting curriculum content both in the field instruction phase and in the rest of the curriculum components. (3) There ought to be contact with the rest of the agency and/or institution staff to make them aware of the university's goal and may share their knowledge in developing a relevant educational experience. (4) University liaison should not be limited to those agencies and/or institutions where students have field placements. Liaison must also be developed with a variety of users of B.A. social workers. Such communication needs to be developed if undergraduate education is to be relevant to the changing needs of society.

The issue confronting our society today demands liaison with the various groups in society who will be the recipients of social work services. This is especially necessary with groups whose value systems and life styles differ from middle class America. Just having representatives of such groups on a consulting committee will not be enough. In fact, this may not achieve the desired goal. Instead, such groups ought to be brought into the educa-tional experience of the students. For example, a university could employ as teaching assistants on a part time basis Chicanos, welfare mothers, Puerto Ricans, and Indians, to mention a few, to help students interpret or become sensitive to the meaning of words, behaviors and value systems of such client groups or communities when examining specific case histories or devising societal interventive programs. Similar kinds of involvements need to be arranged at various points in the curriculum. Evidence also indicates that this ought to happen even when teaching minority groups in social work education.

Another area in which educational institutions that offer undergraduate programs need to creatively work is to sell their product to employers. Though there is adequate evidence that B.A. social workers function exceed-ingly well in many settings where graduate social workers have been required up until now, and though there is ample evidence to show that B.A. social workers will function much better than other B.A. graduates; yet government personnel boards and private agencies have not been able to clarify social work functions adequately to develop career ladders that coordinate the degree of social work education and/or experience with various levels of the career ladder.

Some efforts have been made in workshops or conferences sponsored by the Council on Social Work Education, the Southern Regional Education Confer-ence, and the Western Interstate Commission on Higher Education at national, regional, and state levels, however progress has been slow. Efforts must be

23

made at local and state levels by colleges and universities to solve this void in effective program implementation. Undergraduate social work faculty must bring together agency/institution employers and state personnel boards. Another important factor in opening doors for B.A. social workers is in the effective work done by students in field instruction. Evidence indicates this is the most effective way of selling a good product. A good product, however, depends on a good educational program.

At the same time, however, efforts must be made to create new areas of employment for our students. In America today new structures are coming into being that require the expertise and the kinds of services that the B.A. social worker is able to provide. Urban coalitions, local, regional and state planning agencies, activist groups, community and neighborhood organizations, occupational organizations, industry and other business organizations, among others, are work opportunity settings where what the social worker can do for their programs or activities needs to be explored.

At the present time job opportunities for B.A. social workers are not the best. Tight budgets is one factor. But one must also remember that little is known about present manpower needs. Everyone should also be aware of the fact that government services, the largest service area for social workers, have been in a state of flux. At the moment the scene reflects a viewpoint that economic security will solve all ills.

It has been six years since the last manpower study. Conditions today are quite different. An outgrowth of that study is the new research recently begun by the Federal Government. May, 1971, saw the first of a series of reports by the Department of Health, Education and Welfare on social welfare manpower. It is entitled Working Papers No. 1: National Study of Social Welfare and Rehabilitation Workers, Work and Organizational Contexts. In the foreword of this first publication Richard M. Longmire, Associate Administrator for Planning, Research and Training, Social and Rehabilitation Service, states:

"Most public and private social welfare and rehabilitation agencies in the United States today face a basic dilemma: demand for service is growing faster than the supply of manpower needed to supply service. Agencies therefore are finding it imperative to stretch the available supply of workers by using them more effectively and to hire and train new workers from many sources. But almost invariably they find that they lack the knowledge essential to successful accomplishment of these imperatives.

It is for this reason that the Social and Rehabilitation Service has undertaken a five-year program of research on workers in the field, the work they do, and the settings in which the work is performed: the

National Study of Social Welfare and Rehabilitation Workers, Work, and Organizational Contexts. The integrated program is expected to yield more new knowledge for the resources invested than would a large number of independent projects. 21/

It is the intent of the federal government to make the results of these studies known to policy makers, administrators, service delivery workers, and other personnel of public and private agencies and to teachers and students in the field. The year 1973 is the target date for its completion. Undergraduate educators need to keep abreast of these findings if education and work opportunities or structures and functions are to have some semblance of compatibility.

It remains to be seen whether this research on social welfare manpower effort will provide the helping services and the social work world in particular with the kind of information needed to provide appropriate education for the career ladder of the social work delivery system. Dysfunctional relationships already exist in the system that cannot be corrected by just doing a piece of research on the nature of work being performed if employment policies are not adjusted to meet the situations that exist. For example, too many state personnel or civil service boards ignore the fact that B.A. social workers have an expertise not found among other B.A. graduates. As long as differential employment among B.A. graduates is not practiced the educational system and the state delivery systems will be at a point of disjuncture.

Furthermore, first impressions of this research project lead me to feel that it will not be very helpful in determining the nature of services or the kinds of delivery systems required by contemporary society. For example, as long as management goals are to devise the most expeditous ways of providing people with financial security through determination of eligibility and the appropriate kinds of criteria to assess the amount of the check, or even just to determine in a simplified fashion what the person's economic situation is to bring his financial state up to a certain minimal level, then the analysis of the kinds of services needed will provide an answer just for that kind of goal. But what if, in fact, the goal ought also to include the delivery of other kinds of social services. Then the analysis of service delivery personnel and systems changes. And it seems that this will not be part of the goal of this research.

As undergraduate social work education matures, it has an obligation to contribute to a body of knowledge that will help provide for society the kind of services and the types of delivery systems necessary to meet the social service needs of today.

21/

Department of Health, Education and Welfare, Social and Rehabilitation Services, Working Papers No. 1: National Study of Social Welfare and Rehabilitation Workers, Work, and Organizational Content. (Washington,D.C.: Superintendent of Documents, U.S. Government Printing Office, 1971), p. iii

CONCLUSION

Undergraduate social work education has come into being. Qualified educational personnel, curriculum development, educational methodologies and structures, and research for the appropriate delivery of services demand its attention. Dr. Arnulf Pins has correctly noted that we are "at a time when major re-examination and restructuring of the entire curriculum in undergraduate social welfare education is being undertaken." 22/ The times call for the best that schools who now join the ranks of approved members are able to provide. For society demands relevant education that will provide B.A. social workers with the expertise commensurate to the task.

22/
    Loewenberg and Dolgoff, op. cit., p. iii.

PART II: PAPERS DEVELOPED FROM THE WORKSHOP

THE PROS AND CONS OF USING A CURRICULUM
IN UNDERGRADUATE FIELD INSTRUCTION

by

Serapio R. Zalba*

The term curriculum is Latin in origin, and it refers to a race track--
a prescribed course over which a race is run. Educators and students alike
are concerned that educational curricula actually will regiment them so that
they might have to run through a prescribed (race) course of study--a curri-
culum--which allows little or no room or time for development of their
individual tastes, needs or aptitudes, and little chance to notice and enjoy
the intellectual and professional scenery they encounter on the way.

To what extent should field instruction be (a) a race on a closed course,
(b) a guided group tour through relatively new territory, (c) an individual
exploration with an experienced guide, or (d) a personal trip with a know-
ledgeable native available for guidance? Are there outstanding features,
history, legends, facts, which all visitors should know about if they are to
appreciate their passing through the territory? Is there sufficient time,
or must time be protected as a matter of high priority, for the visitor--the
student--to follow his own interests, and his own priorities? Does the value
of a guide--a teacher--become apparent only after the visitor has experienced
the limitations and frustrations of a short term of unguided travelling?

Pursuing the basic question of whether or not a curriculum should be
used in undergraduate field instruction programs, even metaphorically, requires
some identification of the goals--long range, intermediate, and short term--
for field instruction, and some discussion of how students learn and of how
teachers can help them in that endeavor.

OBJECTIVES OF FIELD INSTRUCTION

The objectives as determined by the teacher are not always the objectives
of the student. If learning of any real import is to take place, the goals
of both teacher and student must overlap to some significant extent; otherwise,
little learning that will meet the needs of both parties will take place.

*Serapio Zalba is Chairman of the Social Service Department, Cleveland State
University, Cleveland, Ohio.

Program Goals

From the perspective of the teacher, including the program and the university he represents as well as of social work education in general, the goals most typically enunciated are the following:

1. Preparation for direct services employment. This is one of the emerging goals of undergraduate programs in social work, social services and human services. It is expected that completion of the undergraduate sequence will prepare students for entry into direct service positions in human services occupations, especially if the programs meet the standards set by the Council on Social Work Education.

2. Preparation of students for entry into graduate schools of social work. In some cases it is expected that beginning professional skills will be gained only at the graduate school level. Other undergraduate programs have as their primary goal the preparation of students as beginning professionals with the understanding that the completion of graduate school will make them ready for more advanced practice. It is also expected that additional training in administrative and research skills will be provided by graduate studies.

3. Enhancement of the "quality of life." Many programs located in liberal arts colleges hope to influence the quality of life of the communities in which their students will live. More specifically, they hope that their students will develop strong, knowledge-based concern for their fellow man, with a clear understanding of the major contemporary problems of their society, and a rational approach toward addressing the community problems which are a part of their burden as citizens. At the very least they would want to sensitize students to the effects of war, environmental pollution, racial injustices, the widespread use of drugs, and other social problems on society and on its citizens.

The four universities and Veterans Administration hospitals which participated in the Undergraduate Field Experience Demonstration Project shared these objectives with varying priorities. The North Carolina unit team gave highest priority to Objective 1; the New York team gave equal priority to Objectives 1 and 2; Washington State gave top priority to Objective 1 but also stressed Objectives 2 and 3; Minnesota gave precedence to Objective 2 but also addressed itself to Objectives 1 and 3.

There is disillusionment among some members of the social work profession and among many students toward the traditional professions. They have witnessed professionals placing primary emphasis on their own personal interests; that is, careerism, consequently acting in ways detrimental to the clients whose interests they are there to serve. In response to this feeling some undergraduate programs direct themselves to helping students develop a truly professional approach toward their work, not necessarily identifying with any one established profession. A professional approach might be characterized as follows: (a) effectiveness in service, (b) pride of accomplishment, (c) skill in practice, (d) a responsible, autonomous, and ethical approach to one's work, (e) knowledge about one's area of work, including up-to-date theory, techniques and programs, (f) a stance of curiosity, and willingness to learn and use all of what one knows in one's practice, and (g) a value perspective about the relative importance of various considerations in the society and in one's own practice. I would contrast this general approach with the socialization into professions which typically occurs, and which frequently carries with it self-serving aspects that come to have a higher priority than is publicly acknowledged or sanctioned.

Students' Goals

As we listen to students talk about their aspirations for pursuing an education, certain phrases occur over and over again. Among the major ones are, for example, the quest for personal identity. Another is the desire to help one's fellow man and to develop a greater sense of community and personal concern. A third is to improve the total society which is seen as being imperfect, the blame for which often is attributed to the failure--moral and social--of the older generation. This latter perspective creates a problem for the student who, at this stage in his life, typically is seeking to reconcile his own needs for independence and competence with his family and societal heritage, often seen in conflict.

In the contemporary language of students, these goals are part of "doing their own thing." Their motivations are obviously related to Maslow's formulations of self-realization, self-esteem, and affection needs. In today's affluent society the safety and physical needs of most students have been met to the extent that they are less salient as motivators for a college education than was true in the past. Students seem to be seeking primary meaning for their lives in terms other than career success and financial reward. Instead they seem to be seeking congruence of thought, action and values--typically humanistic values. They are very impatient of those persons whose behavior seems unauthentic or incongruent (to use terms popularized by Carl Rogers).

These student goals echo, to some degree, community mental health concepts which teach that help can be and should be provided at one's own doorstep from one's own relatives, neighbors, and friends, as well as from local need-meeting societal agents. The skill of helping, and the commitment to help, from this perspective, are seen as a social responsibility of community membership, rather than solely as a professional one. From this point of view, field instruction could be regarded as a liberal educational experience in responsible, educated citizenship. At the same time, the values that have been described above are consistent with professionalism in the most positive sense rather than in the self-serving careerism sense.

This is not to say, however, that undergraduate social work programs must be located in liberal arts colleges, or that they cannot or should not be professional in their focus or orientation. There are successful undergraduate social work programs found in professional schools.

It is no paradox that many of our students, while wanting to be relevant, authentic, and caring, still hope to develop saleable skills which allow them in many cases to move from working class backgrounds into professional middle-class status. The desire for mastery at this stage of personal development is consistent with the development of professional skills. It is, moreover, consistent with professional pride of accomplishment, responsibility, and concern.

TEACHING TOWARD GOALS

Teaching methods used by teachers of social work practice can be categorized into four types:

1. Incidental teaching--the teacher pursues the content introduced by the student.

2. Opportunistic teaching--the teacher picks and chooses from those experiences described by the student, taking advantage of learning experiences as they occur.

3. Anticipatory teaching--the teacher, on the basis of his experience, anticipates that certain key issues will emerge in practice. He will take advantage of practice incidents illustrating basic problems and issues which are believed to be of importance for anyone wanting to become a social worker.

4. Planned teaching--the teacher takes responsibility for introducing content and concepts, generating specific experiences which will induce learning in the directions which the teacher has planned beforehand.

If one is to pursue the idea of a curriculum, it would seem that the latter two types of teaching--anticipatory and planned teaching--would be the modes most amenable to the building of a curriculum. If a teacher is to plan for the kind of learning which he hopes to induce, he must have some control over the kinds of experiences which the student will encounter in field instruction, although he may need to supplement these through exercises or simulations in order to prepare the students for subsequent experiences in the field. There is a fine line of distinction between the grouping of incidental and opportunistic teaching and anticipatory and planned teaching. The essence of the difference is that the former grouping does not represent a curriculum while the latter does. Yet opportunistic and anticipatory teaching are similar in that they employ a similar teaching approach where the student is helped to digest his experiences through class assignments, discussion, conferences, analyses, logs, papers, presentations, etc. This leads to the inductive generation of basic concepts that can provide some guidance for future practice. These concepts would need to be identified and integrated into theoretical frames of reference and cognitive maps to help the budding practitioner.

Classroom learning designs have been moving away from the straight lecture method; 1/ they have become similar to the field instruction which students for many years have reported as the most significant learning experience in the social work concentration. The experience in the classroom has been that preparation for practice seems to be much more effective, exciting, and productive, when it proceeds from a base of experience on the part of the student. The experience can be induced through group tasks, through simulations, and through real task assignments such as research, students helping one another in relationships within the classroom as in the Gestalt method, etc. There is, however, a curriculum component in the decisions that must be made as to when experiences should be introduced and how they should be handled. There are basic questions as to timing. There are decisions as to what content to introduce and when, and at what points the learning should be deductive rather than inductive. How much of the material of practice can be presented in the classroom as anticipatory preparation for the field? How much of the theory would be absorbed better if it were presented after the fact, in order to help explain already experienced practice field phenomena?

WHOM DO WE TEACH?

It is clear that our students represent wide divergences in personal life goals, prior experiences, maturity, motivation, and skills. Some students come from extremely stable family backgrounds with strong personal identities and are able to withstand the frustrations inherent in trying to help troubled people. Other students have a much greater need for immediate fulfillment and

---

1/

Recent Annual Program Meetings of CSWE reflect this trend. See, also: Ohmer Melton, "Teaching or Learning?", Research Report Number 6, American Association for Higher Education, Washington, D.C. (May, 1971).

33

positive feedback. These students are likely to require more immediate results in their work with clients. They would more frequently experience distress in working with other people.

Students also have differing tolerances for the kinds of clients and problem situations they can deal with. It requires educational as well as interpersonal sensitivity to help a student learn to work with the poor, with older people, with acting-out youth, or with persons who have psychiatric and medical problems. Our task is then to explore, with the student, the extent and meaning of his reactions to certain types of clients, so that we might plan with him a program which would de-sensitize him to certain kinds of currently disabling situations.

This is not an argument for an "educational diagnosis"--a term which I dislike and find fraught with ambiguities as to the roles and goals of both teacher and student. Indeed, the preferred strategy would be to build upon the strengths of the student's motivations. But unless the student has a good background in social work knowledge to begin with, there, will be under-developed capacities and talents. The ability to be comfortable with, and helpful to a larger range of clients, may be contingent on greater famili-arity, contact, and knowledge of the social work field. For example, there are students who never even consider certain placements such as hospital work, who, upon exploration with the field work coordinator, accept such a placement, thrive on it, and later seek and find employment in such place-ments. This frequently happens in the fields of work with the aged and in corrections.

In addition, this also happens with regard to group work or community organization programming. If the student has had little or no experience with a particular practice method, he may not seek such experiences, es-pecially if there is little provision to help him with feelings of awkward-ness, apprehension, and lack of skill. Some programs make an effort to have students gain some experience in working with face-to-face groups and community action groups as well as in one-to-one situations. This is a curricular decision and implies the design and use of a curriculum.

The curriculum guide designed by the New York unit, for example, included both the use of "more than one method, and exposure to more than one kind of problem area." The students in that program worked with clients on both a one-to-one and a group basis. In addition, they had the opportu-nity of familiarizing themselves with work in geriatrics, rehabilitation of the blind, and medical clinics, as well as in day treatment for psychiatric patients. The North Carolina curriculum guide plans for student experience with individuals, with groups and in community organization.

The issue becomes clearer if we consider some of the students we see, with their differing readiness to move into helping roles. As I think about some of the students I have taught, I recall one student who had been working for approximately three years on a part-time basis--as a teacher, a group worker, and a student-leader in a foreign travel work experience--whom we were able to move very quickly into independent leadership helping roles and even place in a psychiatric emergency suicide prevention clinic for field instruction. Arrangements have been made for him to take some doctoral level courses in another program at a nearby university concurrent with his work to complete his baccalaureate degree. Contrast this with other students from relatively protected environments, with limited first hand contacts with persons of other ethnic origins, with persons of lower socio-economic class, or poverty situations, whose experiences in a field instruction program would be among their first with persons with serious problems. How do the learning needs of a student who has been active in organized youth leadership programs in middle class community centers contrast with those of another student, a bit older, who has worked for many years, has knowledge about the drug scene from firsthand experience, and is street-wise about problems that are not typical of middle class clientele? Consider if you will, two young ladies, one from a minority group, who has been working in a public welfare manpower project and has had extensive work experience, with another young lady with high motivation and a real concern for people, but no work experience, and with little personal contact with persons in serious problem situations.

The intellectual capacities, energy levels, and personalities of students also must be taken into consideration when developing educational goals and planning learning activities with them. Students with physical disabilities and low energy levels present a different challenge from the vibrantly aggressive, healthy student ready to run off in any number of directions, with vigor, and interest, and skill. We have had students with psychiatric disabilities who have overcome them, whose experiences have made them very sensitive to certain problem areas that an inexperienced student would have great difficulty in understanding. Such illustrations serve to dramatize the fact that students do not start field instruction from the same beginning point. Previous to placement some have considerable paid work experience in dealing with people on a helping basis. Some have much greater sensitivity and awareness of a variety of societal problems than do others, and, they do not learn in the same way.

These factors lead me to conclude that there needs to be an individualized curriculum for each student. The task, basically, then, is to develop the kind of curriculum that will provide students the opportunity to confront the types of practice issues that will face them later as workers and to develop the kind of expertise that is not limited to the setting in which it was learned. We must provide the kinds of learning activities that will enable students to achieve these educational goals. Such an approach is concretized in the curriculum guides developed by the four units that participated in this project.

Who Teaches?

Another variable to be taken into account when considering what will be learned by the student in field instruction is the field instructor himself, with the knowledge, skills, attitudes, awareness, and personal style he brings to his task. What is the permeating philosophy of the teacher and the program? Is learning conceived as a recipient process-- where one with greater knowledge transmits to the one with lesser knowledge? Or is it a more cooperative or collaborative process?

Is designing a curriculum for a student a common task in which the teacher and student alike are involved? Can the learning needs of the student be anticipated to some extent? Can field instruction be predesigned even though alterations will need to be made when the specific student is taken into consideration? And, who makes the specific placement? Do students decide which agencies they wish to be placed in as they do in some programs or are they referred to an agency jointly chosen with the field coordinator, where they meet with a prospective field instructor to determine whether such an arrangement would be mutually satisfactory and beneficial? Are they asked to indicate the field of service in which they are interested or are they placed in an agency based upon the unilateral decision of the faculty? The New York program, for instance, asked the student to state his preferred field, and then arranged for the student to meet with the agency field instructor before making a final decision as to his agency placement.

One approach to this problem is to begin the process of making field placement decisions as early in the student's career as a social work major as possible. We need to know in some detail what the student's educational and professional assets and deficits are. We need to know their career aspirations. We need to know about their learning style and their work habits, their fears and their preferences.

Once that information has been gathered we can plan with the student for the kind of placement to be made. It is true that specific placement is limited by the agency slots that have been provided for and which are currently available. However, some students have initiated contact with new agencies and helped to develop new placements or have used other innovative means to expand the choice of placements. In some programs, as indicated above, students meet with their potential field instructor during the quarter before field instruction begins, so that student and field instructor might become acquainted, and advise if either party is uncomfortable with the arrangement. This also affords the student the opportunity to do some reading in anticipation of field instruction.

Many students have been very willing, and indeed anxious to prepare themselves in this way. Some agencies have even invited their prospective students to attend staff meetings, staff training sessions, case consultations, etc. Students have found that this eases their entry into the agency and gives them a greater sense of identification with the agency prior to actual entry. It also gives some greater depth to a placement which is typically seen as extremely time-limited as is true with many current programs. The question of the actual length of time for field instruction is a crucial curriculum issue which is discussed later in this paper.

TEACH FOR WHAT PURPOSE?

One of the major issues in designing a curriculum for field instruction has to do with the kind of practice that will be taught, both in terms of techniques and in terms of objectives and strategy. Do we try to prepare the student to think and behave in the same way as those currently employed in the agencies where placements are available? Are we attempting to anticipate some of the trends in practice and in techniques which may be more modern and more effective? Do we believe that we can enhance the quality of social services provided in our communities by preparing our students to serve in new and innovative ways which are not yet common in the agencies which might hire them? These are very serious questions which have important educational implications.

There is another consideration in the linkage between classroom and field. How well do the two areas articulate and even collaborate? Does what is learned in the classroom adequately prepare the student for practice in the field instruction placement? Do classroom and field instructors utilize consistent interventive strategies, techniques, objectives and conceptualizations? Recurrent difficulties have been experienced by all participants--field instructors, classroom instructors, and, most of all, students. There are ways of mitigating the perhaps inherent discontinuity among individual instructors, whether classroom to classroom, classroom to field, or from one agency to another. One solution--relatively successful in some programs--has been to hold ongoing seminars where field and classroom instructors discuss the content they are teaching and the methods they use. 2/ The result is that field and classroom instructors have developed a much greater appreciation for each other's role. Classroom instructors are invited to agencies and field instructors are invited to visit, participate, and even teach some classes.

2/

This general approach--of bringing field faculty into close contact with the classroom--is described in detail in the North Carolina curriculum guide.

A major concern has been to avoid putting the student in the position where he must divide his loyalties between university and agency. Instead the objective is to open communications and learning possibilities so that classroom material can be tested and discussed in the field, while agency experiences are utilized in classroom learning. Universities must work with agency instructors and utilize those agencies that will allow their students some latitude in exploring differing practice techniques and strategies.

While wanting to be innovative, we must realize that it is a cruel deception to a student to socialize him to a way of practice and a way of thinking which will interfere with the likelihood of his being hired. We hope we are practical in this respect. But it is likewise cruel to socialize a student into a helping system which is known to be ineffective and which must, of necessity, change in the near future.

Some undergraduate programs seek to prepare their students to work with people in a variety of different employment settings and roles, rather than solely within the traditional social work field. Their aim is to enable students to develop skills in helping others, which will prepare them to enter into various fields, including vocational rehabilitation, manpower development and placement, corrections, medical social service, neighborhood centers, child welfare agencies, etc.

HOW DO PEOPLE LEARN?

It is obvious to anyone who has been involved in educational activities that there are a variety of personal learning styles. One of the major differences is that which exists between active and passive learner. In some subject matter disciplines it may be acceptable for students to be passive in their approach to learning, but in social work education the student should learn to become an active learner so that he can develop an active mastery over the content. This supports the value position that a student must learn to become responsible for his own learning after his formal education has been completed. To facilitate this we should design situations in the classroom as well as in the field where individual students, or groups of students will eventually have some responsibility for developing content to be presented to others in the class as part of their learning experience.

Another dimension in personal learning styles has to do with inductive versus deductive learning. It is possible to operate from the premise that learning is meaningful only when it provides a solution to one's personal dilemma--that is, meets one's needs. This leads to a bias in favor of inductive learning, whereby the concepts and the generalizations are conclusions drawn from the data of one's own experiences. This position is consistent with the phenomenological approach towards the determination of what is true. This issue will be discussed later. Closely related to the inductive/deductive issue is the dimension of "here and now" learning versus anticipatory learning and retrospective learning. My bias is to work with students toward helping them develop the capacity to learn from their "here and now" experiences. 3/ This involves helping them to develop awareness of their own responses to experiences and learning to assess, with some degree of accuracy, the responses of others to those same experiences. 4/ This does not negate the value of some anticipatory learning. It seems quite clear that the anxiety of the student before his first interview with a client can be allayed to some extent by role-playing with him in order that he might get the "feel" of what he might do during a real interview. There is a here-and-now quality to role playing, even if it is a simulation in anticipation of a real situation in the future. As part of the inductive approach to learning, there must be retrospective examination of experiences with a view toward elucidating principles and theoretical formulations from those experiences. This is not inconsistent with the position that one must become as aware as possible of what one is experiencing at the time of crucial transactions. As the student becomes aware of his own responses, thoughts, and actions, he can store those data which offer him an empirical test of the formulations, abstractions, and generalizations so that they can serve as guides to his professional behavior at any later point in his career.

Good communications, and good learning requires alternating between levels of abstractions. Firsthand behavioral experiences should be alternated with some summarizations or deductions about the meaning of those experiences. Analysis and assimilation should follow experiential inputs; these should be followed by feedback to the action system.

Crisis theory suggests that it is at the moment of greatest need, of the immediacy of need, that one is willing to consider novel solutions and alternative behaviors vis-a-vis the presenting problem. The application of this principle to an educational context suggests that it is only as the student has need for a concept or a theory that he will be receptive and indeed alert to the meaning of the implications of principles and theories.

In summary, the basic position taken here is that people learn experientially, and that abstractions such as principles, concepts, and theories affect behavior to the extent that they are arrived at inductively from an

---

3/

This approach is strongly emphasized in the Washington State curriculum guide.

4/

The self-awareness dimension of social work learning was prominent in the curriculum guides of all four units where it was stated as a specific learning objective.

experience base or are corroborated by experience. In addition, the willingness to consider abstract ideas is related, to a great extent, to the need one has because of one's current real situation and for the value which those ideas will have in the solution of concrete problems.

What is True?

Social work as a practice field is of necessity pragmatic--things are true insofar as they are true in practice. This stance leads to a phenomenological approach toward the determination of what is true and what one's theoretical knowledge base for practice will be. The basic phenomenological position is as follows: Truth is not determined by "objective" empirical evidence but is a subjective perception of reality, which provides a basis for behavior and action to the extent that the conception being advanced is consistent with the experiences by the individual would have been screened or monitored in such a way so as to be seen as consistent with, supported by, or explained by the concepts or theories being advanced. While it is true that a theory may sensitize an individual to conceptualize or organize his experiences in a new way, it is also true that it is the human experience itself that will eventually lead the individual to accept a theory and to make it part of his cognitive organization.

The processes by which students develop cognitive maps are many. Included are the following:

1. The student may discover certain consistencies or patterns on the basis of his own experience.

2. He may need help from a teacher, or from his peers to discern the regularities in his experiences that allow him to predict and control behavior in the future.

3. He may learn from the experiences of others. This may be on the basis of his trust for the others, and his willingness to tentatively accept their version of the meaning of their experiences, or it may involve a sympathetic resonance to the experience of others which awakens his own experiences, and allows him to draw conclusions from those experiences.

4. Another mode of learning is to extrapolate from one's own prior experiences and try to determine what one would feel or how one would respond if certain additional experiences were encountered.

5. Another alternative or substitute for one's own real experiences is to walk through--role play--typical kinds of experiences that occur in one's practice. In the process of role playing it is possible to generate real emotions and reactions to situations which will be confronted in the field. Related to this approach is the use of individual and interpersonal exercises in which actual situations are set up where engagements generate real feelings and reactions which can then be examined.

Some examples of experientially-induced learning in the classroom may be of interest. In courses on interpersonal relations, which are sometimes required as part of the development of the professional helping potential of the students, students are exposed to a variety of interpersonal exercises designed to help them get a clearer view of those areas in which they may have difficulties. One such exercise is called "the trust walk"; students are paired off, one taking the role of the helper, and the other closing his eyes and being guided as though he were blind. The experience of being led by someone you do not know very well, when you cannot see what is happening to you, provides a dramatic confrontation of one's ability to place one's trust in the integrity and skill of another person. This exercise typically results in exciting and significant learning on the part of the student. There are other exercises that can be utilized in the classroom which are related to interviewing, recording, aggression, entry, termination, etc. 5/

Admittedly a great deal of stress has been placed on the experiential aspect of learning. While a maximum of information can be transmitted through highly structured communications, such as lectures or reading assignments, it is problematic whether information gained in such ways will become personalized and integrated so that it will significantly influence behavior. It is our belief that the student is much more likely to be influenced in his behavior by ideas which he has arrived at through his own processes and which are based on his own experiences, than on the hearsay of others' experiences which the student has not personally validated.

BUILDING INDIVIDUALIZED CURRICULA

The unique nature of field instruction as a learning device lies in its ability to put into practice the concept of learning through doing and through serving, as advocated by John Dewey. This position is neither anti-intellectual nor anti-theoretical. A basic mission of such a program is to help the student develop cognitive maps, as well as practice skills, self-awareness, and a disciplined use of self and skills. A scientific aspect of practice, and perhaps one of its artistic attributes as well, is the ability of the practitioner to predict the outcome of his behaviors, and to order and choose alternative behaviors on the basis of conceptual and theoretical frameworks. The development of this capacity is a major goal of the field instruction component of the social work curriculum.

In the curriculum guides developed by those who participated in the Undergraduate Field Experience Demonstration Project it is clear that some important conceptual and cognitive maps had been explored with students. For example, several participating units identified the necessity for the student to consider his agency and its program in social system terms.

5/

A program of psychodrama was used much in this way as shown in the curriculum guide developed by the Washington State unit team.

The use of this frame of reference provides the practitioner with a perspective that allows him to understand and predict events that otherwise
would seem chaotic and random. The same holds true for organizational
theory. It seems obvious that a person operating in a complex organization
would need to have some conceptual landmarks by which he might guide his
behavior and predict the outcome of alternative courses of action available
to him.

There are ways to solve the problem of designing curricula which
introduce concepts in a sequence that would make for maximum learning by
the student. 6/ The position taken here is that individualized curricula
should be designed for each student participating in field instruction.
These curricula should be designed in accordance with some general principles which will be described below. The underlying principle, however,
is to follow the normal flow of anticipated experiences which the student
will undergo as he enters into, and later completes field instruction.

The first stage will be the student's anticipations prior to actual
placement, related to the individual's fears, dreams, and actual expectations. Accordingly, it is possible to take advantage of this natural
concern to have the student and his field instructor work together toward
a learning plan for that student. Part of the student's task in this
process is to assess his or her own position with regards to career goals,
learning and professional assets, current deficits, prior experiences, etc.
Some of this process begins prior to actual placement in a specific agency
for field instruction. The process begins with the student meeting with
the field work coordinator, and continues as a specific placement agency
is proposed to the student. Once the student and the field instructor
agree that they want to work together, they can make an inventory of assets,
liabilities, prior experiences and personal career goals, and attempt to
write out specific learning goals against which performance at the end of
field instruction will be measured. This is a process which allows the
assessment of the relative success or failure of any program for a specific
student. In other words, we would follow a strategy of instruction by
specific objectives.

Entry

The major themes at the point of entry into field instruction are
parallel by the experience of the client entering the agency. The student
is, therefore, sensitive to the problems of entry into new situations,
especially service and learning situations. 7/ A student's learning at this

_____

6/
  The Minnesota unit did this with a sequence of factual content, problem-
  solving and inventive content, and self-understanding and awareness content.

7/
  With both the Washington State and North Carolina units students in field
  instruction went through some regular patient procedures as a sensitization
  experience.

time can be built upon his sensitization to these issues. It is anticipated that themes such as fear and uncertainty regarding demands and
expectations of persons in power positions, concerns about rejection and
acceptance, and about one's capacity to help one's self and others, will
be foremost at this time. The curriculum in the field can be designed
to pursue these issues at the times it is clear they are operative. If
the student does not initiate them in his learning conferences with his
field instructor, it may be expected behavior on the part of the teacher
that he will introduce these issues with the student. This allows the
student to become aware of the typicality of the experiences which he
and his fellow students go through in field instruction.

Data Collection

The next stage in the student experiences has to do with collecting
data about one's situation and the context in which one finds oneself.
Stress is placed on the effects and importance of historical data on the
current circumstances, organizational and otherwise, in which clients
find themselves, and on their roles, personalities, etc.

Trust

As the student makes contact with agency personnel and with clients,
interpersonal trust becomes an issue. Here, again, the themes of trust,
and of how trust is developed, and of the consequences of trust or lack
of it, and of the risks involved, are topics of high valence at this
point of time.

Plan of Action

A next stage involves consideration of the data and its analysis so
that it will provide some understanding of the current situation and some
guidance as to the strategies and actions that might be appropriate in
work with the client. Again I am assuming that this is parallel to the
student's own consideration of his situation in field placement.

It is anticipated that with help from his field instructor he will
develop a plan of action which outlines the learning that he hopes will
take place and which he commits himself to pursue during his field instruction. 8/ This is the phase that could be labeled the "contract phase,"
where student and teacher clarify their expectations of one another and
lay out a plan of action for the work they will be doing together.

8/
This idea is well developed in the Washington State curriculum guide.

43

Work Themes

The next step in the process involves the work which is the basic reason for bringing together student and teacher, and worker and client. The work includes the development of practice skills; it also involves the pursuit and understanding of problem themes. These themes may vary according to the setting; they are certainly individualized, in that the pattern of themes particular to one person--student or client--tend to be an individual expression of his personality and his life, but they are recurrent, and must be recognized and dealt with in a succession of cases. An example of some of these themes, as William Schwartz 9/ calls them, are trust, dependency, intimacy, sexual identification, authority, aggression, loss of control, loneliness and mourning, death, dismemberment, etc. 10/ In addition to themes, learning needs to occur in the areas of worker roles, of transference and counter-transference, and other specifics having to do with the provision of services to clients.

As the themes emerge in work with clients, and as the teacher is sensitized to recognize the thematic content of the student's work with his clients, it is possible to help the student recognize the value of considering the experiences of others in working out such themes with different kinds of clients. This can lead to explorations in the literature, to consultation, and to the consideration of the experiences of other practitioners and consultants in the agency and the university. Part of the learning process in the field, and indeed in subsequent professional practice, is the collection of data about the outcome of one's interventions by means of feedback from the client (and from the instructor), and consequent re-evaluation of one's own practice, leading to possible modifications in practice strategy and techniques.

Termination

As the student prepares to leave the agency and terminate his contact with his clients it is timely for him to consider the themes of termination and separation, which are recurrent, and which can be anticipated in any helping relationships.

The student himself will experience separation phenomena as field instruction ends; he will experience many of the same concerns and longings that his clients will as they terminate their contact with one another. Here again, the ground is laid for the student to learn from his own experiences which are related in process to those of his clients.

9/

William Schwartz, "Introduction: On the Use of Groups in Social Work Practice," in William Schwartz and Serapio R. Zalba, eds. The Practice of Group Work (New York: Columbia University Press, 1971), pp. 3-24.

10/

The Minnesota curriculum guide, for example, specifies the themes of aging and poverty among others.

As part of the learning process, there is final evaluation and feedback from instructor to student, and perhaps from student to instructor as well. The student might be asked to evaluate his learning in the field placement, to report to the instructor those acts, behaviors, assignments and experiences which were of particular help to the student, and those which were not helpful. Students might also be asked to make recommendations for the following year. While it is obviously difficult for both teacher and student to give direct and open feedback when there may be some open criticism involved, experience has shown that this can be very helpful to both student and instructor. It is obviously helpful to the program in making judgments as to the agency placements to which it should give precedence in the future placement of its students.

We have identified some specific processes that can be anticipated as the student enters, moves through, and finally completes his field instruction; these parallel many of the experiences of the client as he enters into a relationship with the student, receives services, and finally terminates. The emphasis placed on the student's firsthand experience does not negate the value of certain basic conceptual schema believed to be of value to the student, which might not arise specifically from the problems of his field practice. It seems wise, therefore, to introduce certain substantive areas as we work with students toward understanding their clients, and planning with them to work with the problems brought to the agency. We should take advantage of all opportunities to help the student consider on a case-by-case basis and on a more generalized theoretical basis those things which determine the actions of the client and the outcome of the worker's or student's interventions. Among the topics that might be introduced are motivation, processes of communication, reality factors such as socio-economic circumstances, community conditions, personal health, prior history, family makeup, etc. Such topics are listed in the curriculum guides designed by those universities and agencies that participated in the demonstration project.

Theoretical content can be integrated with practice content by the field instructor when he or she is aware of the relevance of theoretical content and introduces it at the strategic time when it helps to illuminate behaviors of students, their clients, colleagues, etc.

PATTERNS IN PRACTICE EXPERIENCES

We are not suggesting that there should be only one type of field instruction in the undergraduate social work curriculum. Neither do we assume that field instruction should be of the same duration, intensity, or type. Field instruction can even take place before the student has taken formal classroom work in social work or in the interventions portion of the social work sequence. Let us look at some of the possible patterns of learning through practice in the field.

One pattern is to require field instruction during the senior year, after the student has completed his intervention courses. Another pattern is to have two segments of field instruction--one segment to be taken during the junior year; the other during the senior year. There are two major disadvantages to this latter pattern: (1) first the field agencies prefer that the students would have already taken courses on intervention theory, so that the students could use field instruction to learn on a more sophisticated level; (2) the amount of time spent in an agency--for example, eight hours per week for 10 weeks--may not be intensive enough to allow for the learning that the student and the field instructor want to achieve. There is, however, one major advantage to this pattern. If there are two separate segments of field instruction, it is possible to differentiate them so that in the first segment, the junior year, the student is placed in a setting where the prime methods by which help is provided are "clinical"--that is, casework and group work techniques. In the second segment, the following year, on the other hand, students could be placed in agencies where they perform a community organization function. While this does not insure that every student would have had experience with all three levels of intervention--with individuals, with groups, and in the community--it does expose them to at least two of the three levels.

Where there is only one placement the field coordinator may work with the field instructor and the agency executive toward identifying opportunities for students to use multiple methods in field instruction as was evident in the New York and North Carolina curriculum guides. In some cases this may mean that the student has a satellite experience in another agency or in another division of the same agency. If it is at all possible it seems desirable to have students gain experience working with individuals, with face-to-face groups, and in the organization of campaigns and grass roots organizations towards social change, social reform, and social provision. Where personal practice experiences are not possible, we might try to develop opportunities for observation, or consultation related to other methods in which the student himself is not directly engaged.

Feedback from students and from the field instructors in the agencies seems to indicate that we should consider the possibility of extending field instruction during the senior year. Some programs have already experimented by allowing selected students, at their option, to take a second field placement in the same agency. The student thus spends a considerable period of time in one agency. It is conceivable that students might spend an entire school year in field placement on a half-time basis. Other options are that second and third field placements might be taken in different agencies to provide a wider range of experiences from which the student can learn.

46

Some agencies have suggested that students might spend a summer quarter, or perhaps a school year, in full-time placement in an agency. It is another option open to the undergraduate program considering the structural arrangements for field work that would meet the needs of their students and their curriculum. The issue, it should be stressed, is to relate to the specific needs and achievements of the students under consideration. It may be that each program should develop a wide range of alternative field instruction patterns, which then allows them, as a curricula option, to choose that alternative which best meets the needs of any one particular student whom they are placing in the field. This arrangement represents a curriculum design which takes into account the extensiveness of the experiences that can be offered in the field as well as its content.

In some universities and colleges there are courses related to volunteer service in the community. Such courses have two objectives: (1) the liberal arts objective is to allow students the opportunity of involving themselves in the problems of their community, with a view toward helping them gain greater understanding about the meaning of those problems and their effects on people; (2) the professional objective is to afford potential and actual social work majors the opportunity for an early experience in the human services. This provides another opportunity for them to build an experience base upon which to assess concepts presented to them in the classroom. It also gives them a chance to test their commitment to work in the human services. It would be possible to require students without prior direct service experience in the human services to take such a course no later than the junior year, so that as they move toward graduation, there would be less chance that they have commited themselves to a field for which they have no real aptitude or interest. 11/

In addition there are cooperative work experience programs, such as the one at Antioch College. A student, especially in his junior and senior years, can be helped to find a work placement every other quarter so that he alternates a quarter or semester of classroom work with an equivalent amount of time on a job. The job sites and the job roles are selected in such a way as to provide the student with a chance to test his vocational interests and aptitudes in any of a variety of work settings--including social work. However, the tasks assigned to such a worker may be of a very limited kind, and, supervision may not be of the kind or quality available in formal field placements. Among the cooperative work assignments made in the area of social work have been jobs in child care, camp counseling,

---

11/
    The New York curriculum guide provides a strong argument for such career choice testing before commitment to the major.

work with the blind, and work for the boards of education, helping with
disadvantaged children. Such experiences allow the students to test their
vocational commitment to the human services. They also allow them to gain
experiences in working with people in a helping role, which will stand
them in good stead as they later attempt in the classroom and the field to
gain theoretical knowledge about the behavior of people, and try to help
them.

SUMMARY AND CONCLUSION

The essential point when considering the design and use of a curriculum
for the field instruction component of an undergraduate social work program
is that field instruction should be a cognitive experience as well as a
practical experience--one that allows students the opportunity to develop
those personal conceptual schemes and theoretical maps which help him to
find his way in his practice. As the programs of the four units participating in the project demonstrate, it is quite possible to develop a curriculum that is personal yet thorough. His theoretical base should help him
make his choice from among the interventions he might make as a practitioner,
working with the variety of people whom he must serve. At the same time,
it is my conviction that cognitive learning is best achieved as an inductive
process, based on personal experiences. There should be no clear-cut dichotomy
between the learning in the classroom and in the field. The classroom can
be a place where experiences are also generated and explored in a process
toward the development of concepts and principles. This approach is the
Gestalt approach in that we seek to maintain the integrity of experience
in cognitive learning, and the extension of experience into cognitive
learning.

In conclusion, there must, indeed, be the development and use of a
curriculum in undergraduate field instruction. But it is the kind of
curriculum or plan which the group worker makes for a group, in that it
follows natural experiential processes, and provides a variety of options
for the instructor and student. The actual direction in which the process
flows is partly led by the instructor in response to his or her perceptions
of the learning that is taking place. The instructor is prepared by his
or her knowledge of the student and of the typical learning process to
identify the stage of learning at which the student is currently operating,
and the learning opportunities being experienced by the student. The
curriculum is thus seen as a tour through a new territory with an experienced
guide ready to point out the significance of what is being seen, and indeed,
directing the student's attention to some significant features in the landscape which should not be passed unnoticed.

The objective of this journey into the field is the personal growth of the student in the helping role and the integration of his personal growth with his professional skill. He needs to develop his ability to predict the outcome of his interventive behavior, and to order and choose alternative behaviors on the basis of a system of personal and professional values, and of conceptual and theoretical frameworks which guide him.

THE COLLABORATIVE PROCESS IN UNDERGRADUATE
FIELD INSTRUCTION PROGRAMS

by

Kay L. Dea*

Historically, social work education in America has always been closely tied to those formal community agencies sanctioned by society to alleviate personal and community problems related to the structure of man and society. In the 1890s professional schools of social work actually emerged from the apprenticeship programs of social service agencies. As these schools developed and affiliated with universities they maintained agency based field experience as a major component of social work education. This tradition has continued to the present, emphasizing the philosophy that good education allows the student to interact with the society in which he will be living and working.

Justification for field instruction programs, however, goes far beyond a philosophical base which values student learning through life experiences. Pragmatically, such programs serve a variety of utilitarian functions. They provide linkages which enable faculty members to identify changes and trends in practice, to recognize unmet community needs, and to identify unresolved professional issues. When this content is incorporated into a university's curriculum and research efforts, educational programs maintain a vitality and relevancy that assures their survival, accreditation, and acceptance within the community.

At the same time field instruction programs provide opportunities for the infusion of new practice theories and ideas from students and university faculty members to social service agencies. Wayne Vasey has stated that the ivory tower "may offer a commanding view of the professional landscape . . . and a vantage point in detachment from the immediate consequences of practice." [1] University faculty members then, in collaboration with agency staff, may provide new insights into the structure and delivery of agency services.

---

* Kay Dea is a professor at the Graduate School of Social Work, University of Utah, Salt Lake City, Utah.

[1] Wayne Vasey, "The Community Team in Social Work Education: The School," 1956 Proceedings, Education for Social Work (New York: Council on Social Work Education, 1958, p. 30).

Likewise, students who train in agencies bring with them an intellectual curiosity which can stimulate agency staff members to think about new treatment approaches and to continually reassess existing administrative policies and practices. Students may serve as an additional bridge between social agencies and the larger community, interpreting to both lay and professional groups, the policies, strengths, and problems of an agency. They provide agencies with a special manpower pool for the recruitment of staff members who have had professional experience in the actual agency seeking new staff.

To the student himself, field instruction of course provides a structure through which formal theories can be applied to real life. It provides the student with the opportunity to observe and interact with those persons served by community agencies, to work in a collaborative manner with staff members responsible for services, and to develop a personal repertoire of practice skills. Certainly, field instruction **has as a major objective the student's integration of social work knowledge,** skill, and values.

Agency and community involvement in the educational process alone, however, do not necessarily assure for the student this integration nor a valid and effective educational experience. The extent to which field instruction enhances a student's learning is a function of the type of relationship which is established between the university and its field agencies. It is a function of the collaborative process where classroom and field faculty mutually define program objectives for field instruction in relation to a university's educational objectives, a student's individual needs and an agency's specific functions and resources. Community involvement can enrich a university's educational program only as it relates to the educational objectives of the university. Unless field instruction deepens, reinforces, supplements and adds to the content taught in the classroom, field instruction cannot be considered a valid educational part of a university's program. Instead, it becomes an independent, but parallel program in apprenticeship training.

Unfortunately, the long history and rich tradition of field experience in social work education has not automatically resulted in close coordination and cooperation between our campuses and field agencies. To a large extent the ideal cooperative relationships between campus and field have been explicated better in theory than in practice. The coordination of a training program related to two administrative structures and two sets of organizational objectives has frequently resulted in a breakdown of communication and in a confusion of roles. It is to the resolution of these problems from the perspective of an analysis of the collaborative process that this paper is addressed.

HISTORICAL PERSPECTIVES

To some extent the problems currently confronting social work educators in integrating class and field instruction originated at the time social work education shifted from agency apprenticeships to university based programs. This shift required agencies to adopt a new role in the education of students.

In this transition, emphasis was placed upon learning for all social work practice rather than specific tasks and functions in a particular agency. Generic education--preparing students to make complex practical judgments in different contexts and settings--became the primary goal of social work educators. Consequently, this shift had great implications for the role of the agency in providing field training:

(1) It meant that agencies could no longer function autonomously in defining learning experiences, but instead had to rely upon direction from the university in selecting those experiences which supported the "generic objectives" of the educational institution.

(2) It meant that field instructors needed to understand the content, organization, and structure of the university curriculum to reinforce student learning and to provide special assistance in those areas where students have had limited classroom instruction.

(3) It meant that field instructors needed to become concerned with a student's capacity and ability to continually learn--to flexibly develop and change after graduation--rather than exclusively concerned with the specific knowledge and skills students may have possessed at any particular time in relation to the specific functions of a particular agency.

(4) Finally, it meant that field instructors, regardless of their service responsibilities in an agency, had to perceive themselves as educators in their work with students, rather than as service-oriented supervisors. The primary goal of field instruction became generic education rather than agency service and staff development. Consequently, the primary role of the field instructor became that of teaching--not supervising or treating. The primary role of the student apprentice became that of learning--not serving. The role of the agency in field instruction became that of providing educational opportunities and experiences. In this context, agency structure and client services became the media through which learning was achieved.

The maintenance of field experience in social work education also had major implications for universities. Since universities are steeped in academic tradition, these implications have sometimes been ignored.

(1) The placement of students in field work meant that universities could not plan their programs without considering the structure, resources and needs of community agencies, including the relationship of educational programs to an agency's service responsibilities.

(2) It meant that universities had to involve agency staff members in curriculum development and other university activities to assure the latter's understanding of educational programs and to maximize the relevancy of the university in preparing students for professional practice.

(3) Finally, it suggested that the university could not be an ivory tower--pure and neutral in its relations to the political and social problems of the general community. Instead, community based educational programs demand that faculty members commit themselves to a partnership in affecting social changes consonant with the values and ethics of professional practice.

To both the university and the professional agencies involved in social work education the maintenance of field instruction programs required a commitment of time and resources to establish honest, straightforward communication in collaborative relationships which assured a coordination of student learning objectives and the fulfillment of both agency and university goals. The need for adequate communication between campus and field is axiomatic in addressing the educational process in social work.

An analysis of the communication patterns commonly established between universities and social service agencies suggest, however, wide variations in the quality of liaison activities achieved to date. Barbara Varley has stated that cooperation and coordination between campus and field is dependent upon a mutual feeling of trust and confidence. 2/ She has suggested that this trust and confidence can exist only if university and field faculty are identified with one another and committed to the same goals and objectives. This identification cannot occur when agency staff members have the opportunity to know only one or two members of a university faculty or to participate only in field instruction without being involved in other university activities. Similarly, close identification and cooperation are impaired when university faculty members are limited in their contacts with agency staff. The problem, then is one of structuring liaison activities--to maximize contact between the agency and the university, and to facilitate open communication, mutual respect, common goals, trust, and cooperation.

2/ Barbara K. Varley, "The Reciprocal Roles of Campus Teachers and Field Instructors in Educating for Social Work," (mimeographed paper presented at the School of Social Welfare, Florida State University, October 1, 1964).

Traditionally our universities have assigned primary responsibility for coordinating field instruction programs to one or two faculty members. Four basic patterns which have emerged in structuring the frequency and content of relationships between university coordinators and field instructors are identified and discussed below. Although these patterns have not been formally structured, recognized or sanctioned, they have operated informally between the university and each agency involved in field instruction. They may exist alone or in combination with one another, depending upon the unique resources and politics related to each university, agency and respective community. Often, several patterns exist side-by-side within one university.

TRADITIONAL FIELD INSTRUCTION PATTERNS

The four basic patterns which have most frequently emerged in field instruction programs may be classified as follows:

University directed programs:

This pattern is characterized by the university assuming almost exclusive responsibility for defining field instruction objectives and learning experiences consonant with these stated objectives. Communication tends to flow in only one direction--from the university to the agency. Agencies are generally not involved in the selection of students. Agency-based field instructors in this education process are placed in the role of second-class, ancillary teachers.

Although this pattern has the major advantage of safeguarding university direction, thus assuring that classroom theory is reinforced and supplemented in the field, it fails to recognize the contributions that can be made by agency personnel to curriculum development. At the same time it fails to consider agency objectives and needs in defining program goals. Since the university tends to impose its objectives upon agency field instructors, one must question the extent to which this type of pattern fosters mutual identification and commitment to the educational program.

Parallel programs:

This pattern is characterized by little or no communication between the university and the field. Once an agency agrees to train students, the university allows the agency staff complete freedom in defining objectives and in structuring learning experiences. University educators and agency staff members do not work together in developing or sharing field instruction curricula and syllabi. The end result is often an independent "apprenticeship training program" in the field that operates concurrently with the student's university program. It is expected that the learning experiences provided to the student across both programs will be integrated by the student himself. It is also hoped that the two programs are consistent with and support one another. There is no attempt to facilitate integration through the structure of the program.

Although this pattern is not accepted by educators as a sound way to provide field instruction, it often emerges informally as a solution to pressures resulting from the overdemanding time schedules of both the university and agency staff involved. For example, in a recent consultation visit to an undergraduate program in one of the western states, it was found that the director of field instruction (who was also the director of the total program) had never visited several of the agencies where students had been placed. Further, the agencies had not been visited by any university faculty nor had university personnel met the field instructors who were teaching the students. Contacts had been limited to one or two telephone conversations in which arrangements had been made to place students in the agencies. The school had not defined its objectives for field instruction, and agency-based instructors had received no direction from the university. When the director was asked how the program was coordinated he replied, "Until the university gets additional staff there is no time to meet with agency personnel or work on field objectives. We hope the program is integrated by the student through university seminars on field work."

Although agencies may provide excellent training to university students under this pattern, there can be no assurance that the objectives of the university are being met. In those cases where field instruction is weak or in conflict with university goals students will generally be placed in conflict producing situations, with little assistance from the university.

Agency directed programs:

This pattern is characterized by staff members from the agency developing the field curriculum in relation to agency service and objectives. It differs from the parallel pattern, however, in that adequate communication exists between the university and field agencies. Major attention is given to defining the conditions under which agencies will accept students. The responsibilities of students and the university are clearly defined. Primary consideration is given to the service needs of the agency rather than to the educational needs of students. As is true of "parallel programs", different agencies will develop different sets of objectives for field instruction.

55

Again, this pattern is not viewed as educationally sound by university faculty. In a "pure" state it is relatively uncommon, but it develops in individual agencies resulting from limited university-community resources and from political power struggles. When universities take responsibility for clearly interpreting to agencies the educational objectives of field instruction or when they assume a leadership role in developing program objectives in collaboration with agencies, this pattern seldom develops.

Mutually directed programs:

This pattern is characterized by the collaborative involvement of both agency staff members and university faculty members in curriculum development. Frequently joint committees are formed to define university and agency policies regarding field instruction programs. Workshops on a quarterly basis may be held to facilitate communication and cooperative efforts in resolving special problems. Regular contacts are made by the university with agency administrators to assure that both the university and agency are benefiting from the program.

Although this pattern is superior to the other three, it has traditionally been limited to the defining of formal structures and relationships regarding one another's educational responsibilities which in turn remain distinctly separate. Field instructors have served as professional models for practice, providing informal, tutorial learning related to case situations while university faculty have provided basic concepts and principles from social work theory in formally structured classes. Seldom have their roles been reversed or brought into a common, collaborative involvement directed to the specific learning experience of individual students. Instead, collaboration has developed within a narrow and formally defined structure that separates and compartmentalizes student learning experiences into two worlds--the field and the classroom.

In addition, this pattern presents some problems when the structure of the university demands one set of field instruction objectives and learning experiences for all students placed in more than one agency or when university staff resources are inadequate to allow for real collaboration, in the true sense of that term, with each agency. Ideally, the objectives of the field instruction program that is mutually directed by university faculty members and agency staff members must be specifically defined for each agency within the broad context of the university's curriculum and the agency's service responsibilities. Unless this is done the specific needs of either the university or the agency will be ignored in deference to the needs of the other. It is in relation to this point that the CSWE directed and VA sponsored Undergraduate Field Instruction Demonstration Project is unique; namely, in that this project required the collaborative development of field instruction curriculum guides that incorporated both university and agency goals into its program objectives. Unfortunately, this experience has been the exception rather than the rule in social work education. Usually we have established programs emphasizing interaction rather than transaction.

It is my contention, therefore, that none of these four patterns--alone or in combination--provides the ideal framework for collaboration. It is hoped that the problems associated with each of these patterns can be avoided in the future as new field instruction programs emerge in connection with undergraduate education.

A NEWLY EMERGING PATTERN

It is my position that field instruction is most effective when agency staff members and university faculty members develop collaborative relationships based on a transactional model which assures that programs will constantly be adopted in response to the unique and changing configuration of political, economic, social, and cultural spheres in which agencies and universities operate. This pattern requires a true partnership in which the needs of each agency, the university, and the students are constantly reassessed. Then traditional roles of field instructor and university coordinator or instructor will "blur" with much formal teaching occuring in the field and additional experiential learning being presented in the classroom.

This pattern would require that universities recognize that many teachers are not good practitioners and that many practitioners are not effective teachers. Consequently, there could be an interchange of roles enabling each individual to function in his greatest area of competency. For example, classroom and field faculty teams could be assigned to work in teaching centers with perhaps the agency-based individual assuming major responsibility for the development, presentation, and application of formal theory to practice and the university-based individual acting as a "preceptor" in guiding the student through the maze of administrative structures, policies, and programs related to practice, 3/ depending on one another's competencies.

3/

This concept of field instruction was strongly recommended by Professor Bernece Simon at the final workshop held in connection with the Undergraduate Field Experience Demonstration Project in New Orleans, Louisiana, April 29-30, 1971.

This pattern would require that universities assign classroom faculty to work in agency-based teaching centers as individuals or team members responsible for both teaching and agency services. It suggests that a combination of field and classroom teaching assignments could become a basic pattern for social work educators. It also suggests that the university would need to assume greater responsibility for financing and operating field instruction programs. Staffing alternatives that might be developed to achieve the same objectives include the rotation of faculty members through field assignments, staff-exchanges between universities and field agencies, and consortial arrangements in which students are placed in one agency serving several universities with a designated faculty member from one university teaching students from all of the universities.

Regardless of the pattern adopted for the **deployment of faculty,** the position taken in support of this pattern stresses the fact that field instruction encompasses two worlds--the university and agency-- in transaction with one another, rather than in interaction. It suggests that university personnel must be able to "cross over" into the agency world with a basic understanding of the pressures which effect the organization and structure of service programs. It suggests that agency staff members must be able to "cross over" into the world of the university. At the point these two worlds come together, neither university nor agency is seen as existing in a vacuum, but rather both are considered in relation to the larger social and environmental structures in which they operate. Unless social work educators can find ways to function as defined here, there is little hope that we will be able to teach students how to function effectively in transaction with the constellation of social systems to which social work practice must address itself today. Our actions will tend to negate **our** verbal exposé. Our students will be taught to fragment and compartmentalize problems and programs as we fragment and compartmentalize field and classroom learning.

PROBLEMS IN DEVELOPING NEW PATTERNS FOR FIELD INSTRUCTION

But what are the **major** obstacles confronting social work educators in the development of a transactional model for field instruction? What can be done to remove these obstacles? To what extent are they a function of our universities or of our agencies? Among the problems to be addressed are fiscal restraints, academic restraints, philosophical restraints, role restraints, and political and community restraints.

Fiscal Restraints:

Regardless of the pargicular curriculum approach used in field instruction, the involvement of program instructors to cover both university and agency will place pressures upon universities to employ additional staff for field teaching. The current situation in social work education suggests that funds will not be available for this purpose for some time. In addition, fiscal restraints from the field suggest that most agencies cannot employ full-time staff persons to coordinate and administer educational programs. It appears, then, that universities and field agencies will have to improvise to approximate a transactional model in field instruction.

In the meantime, CSWE, NASW and social work educators in general, need to address themselves to the political and economic bodies which control the economic resources for education. If social work educators remain dependent on outside funding for experimental and innovative programs, it is imperative that they find ways to influence those bodies which allocate funds. In developing educational programs we must be careful that constraints occasioned by categorical funding do not destroy the fundamental integrity of a program by adding a rash of new courses and unrelated, uncoordinated projects, or by withdrawing from critical areas and programs which underlie a university's curriculum.

Academic Restraints:

A second problem often confronting social work educators is the general philosophy and orientation of the academic community regarding the whole question of academic vs. vocational training. Many university administrators believe that field instruction programs destroy the academic liberal arts component of undergraduate education. They maintain that any program which prepares students for practice belongs in a vocational school. Although these educators have reluctantly accepted field instruction programs within the undergraduate social work curriculum, they have generally limited the amount of time and resources that a department can invest in these programs to the extent where they remain educationally ineffective. Any intensification of university activities in field agencies will require careful interpretation to university committees and administrators to assure them of the continued academic nature of the program.

Philosophical Restraints:

In addition to considering the basic educational philosophy of the overall university as a variable affecting the development of field instruction programs, social work educators must recognize that their own programs may present philosophical approaches that challenge or conflict with basic positions evidenced by field agency programs and structures. New approaches to either practice or education will most likely demand some modification of already existing positions of both university faculty and agency staff. It is not surprising, therefore, that either or both university and agency faculty may feel threatened by and resist the introduction of new field instruction programs.

Role Restraints:

Regardless of the way in which field instruction programs are structured, the primary role of the university and its faculty members is that of education while the primary role of the agency and its staff members is that of service. Whenever individuals are placed in a dual role, responsible to the goals of both institutions, there is a great potential for role confusion and conflict. Often this conflict takes the form of competition for control of the educational situation. When this happens all parties involved tend to exert pressure to assure that students are programmed in a fashion which assures that one's own objectives will have priority. To the extent that these conflicts exist in social work education, they interfere with the development of close collaborative relationships which should be characterized by open communication, mutual trust, and confidence.

It is imperative that in the development of new programs, responsibilities be clearly defined and delegated for both field and classroom faculty. Unfortunately this is not an easy task when one is developing new collaborative structures in which roles are still evolving. Nevertheless, sound education and administration requires that these responsibilities be negotiated.

Political and Community Restraints:

Finally, both the university and field agencies are subject to a variety of constraints arising out of the larger community in which both function. These constraints may interfere with the development of field instruction programs by imposing limitations on the number and type of agencies that can be involved. The classical example of this type of problem is found where black schools in the South reach out to develop field instruction programs in social service agencies which have traditionally been viewed as "white agencies." Even when black students are accepted into these agencies, universities have found that various forms of discrimination may emerge to limit the type of experiences provided. Similar experiences have been reported by Chicano students in the Southwest. It is imperative that university faculty members and agency field instructors address themselves to these problems in a collaborative manner. As social work educators we must have the courage to demand that agencies operate with policies that are socially just.

Other examples of community restraints are found in politics and religion. In recent years one state commissioner of public welfare informed the directors of all undergraduate programs in his state that universities would not be eligible for public welfare training grants if they placed students in any community agencies for field instruction. It was his contention that field instruction was inappropriate for undergraduate programs.

In another state child welfare agencies operated by a particular church were informed that church policy forbade the assignment of unwed mothers to male caseworkers. When one of the universities affiliated with these agencies protested that male students needed to learn how to work with unwed mothers, the school was informed that its students would have to receive this experience elsewhere.

There are no easy answers to the problems inherent in these examples. Situations such as these, however, suggest that the quality of education provided to social work students very much depends upon the development of collaborative relationships between the community, universities, and field agencies. Certainly there is a need for honest, straightforward negotiation to resolve issues of this nature. At times there may be a need for community censure and confrontation. We cannot expect our students to become agents of social change if we avoid those community situations in which change is needed.

It should be recognized, of course, that the same approach may be needed to achieve changes in the university. Agencies must be free to question the appropriateness of university programs as they are developing. They must be free to negotiate, individually or collectively, formally or informally, with university staff members.

STUDENTS

In all of our work, however, we must not lose sight of the fact that we are primarily responsible to students. They are the immediate consumers of our educational programs. It is they who will be responsible for professional practice tomorrow. Kenneth Boulding has stated:

"It must never be forgotten that the ultimate thing which any society is producing is people. All other things are intermediate goods and all organizations are intermediate organizations. No matter how rich we are or how powerful we are, if we do not produce people who can at least begin to expand into the enormous potential of man, the society must be adjudged a failure." 4/

In our efforts to develop undergraduate social work programs, it is imperative that we recognize that collaborative efforts between university and agency must also take into account the specific needs of the students to be served. As educators we must be aware of the constraints students

---

4/

Kenneth E. Boulding, "Expecting the Unexpected: The Uncertain Future of Knowledge and Technology," Prospective Changes in Society by 1980, Including Some Implications for Education (Denver 1966), p. 213. As quoted in Henry David, "Education for the Professions," Journal of Education for Social Work, Vol. 3, No. 1 (Spring 1967) p. 11.

impose upon the educational system. At the same time we must understand
the social milieu in which students work, study, and play. We must understand the burdens under which they labor--the Kent State's, the Cambodia's,
and the Viet Nam's. We must understand their dreams, ambitions, and
frustrations.

As we work in a collaborative manner to develop educationally-focused
field instruction programs, this attention to students suggests that an
increased emphasis needs to be placed upon independent study and other
approaches to individualized learning. It suggests that in the formal
classroom, as well as the field setting, we need a greater involvement of
students in curriculum development to assure greater relevancy in our
programs. Finally, it suggests that social work educators must become
increasingly adept at utilizing the life experiences which students bring
to the learning situation.

It is hoped that as university faculty and agency field instructors
increasingly accept the challenge to individualize the learning experiences
of each student, collaborative relationships regarding this dimension also
will be developed or maintained, thus facilitating an exchange of information
about each student's needs and the programs to which he has been assigned.
To do less would deprive the student of exciting learning opportunities.

CONCLUSION

In conclusion, it must be recognized that the challenge of developing
more effective patterns of collaboration between our universities and
social service agencies will always be with us. As society evolves and
changes, the structures we establish for university-agency liaison, today,
will soon become obsolete. We must not feel, therefore, that it is our
responsibility to furnish final answers to the problems confronting us.
Rather, we should seek for solutions which provide us with methods and
structures which are flexible and adaptable to change. We should seek
those structures which facilitate mutual trust, respect, honesty, and
common goals between university faculty, agency instructors and students
alike.

If we can develop this type of collaborative relationship between
university and agency--and not necessarily limit to field instruction
programs--social work education will move forward with increased strength
and vitality.

FIELD INSTRUCTION AS EDUCATION FOR PRACTICE: PURPOSES AND GOALS

by

Bernece K. Simon*

This paper is directed toward discussion of some of the important
issues and problems of field instruction as part of the social work
curriculum. The subjects considered in this presentation are those
thought to be fundamental and that were identified as crucial during
the workshop proceedings. Since this paper is a consideration of basic
field instruction issues, the generalizations are derived from experience
with field instruction in the graduate social work curriculum. The ideas
from this experience are offered, not as a model, but as a base from which
work on field instruction in the undergraduate social work curriculum
might develop in many directions. One such direction is suggested in
this paper and was sparked off by the other presentations in the workshop and the spirited discussion of the participants.

Field instruction is a creative invention of social work education
making a unique contribution to students' learning. The nature of its
contribution and the organization and structure of field instruction in
the curriculum lead to perennial problems and issues that require constant
attention, vigilance, and work no matter where in the educational stream
field instruction is found. These issues command attention whenever such
learning is considered central to students' education and whenever what
transpires in the field is considered an essential part of the curriculum.

The questions and issues about field instruction as part of the
curriculum are essentially curricular issues, but with many elaborations
and permutations. These problems may be summarized as follows: purpose
and goal of field instruction, content of field instruction, and method
and format of field instruction. This paper will address these areas as
well as consider some of the current questions about field instruction
that are subject to debate. These currently debated questions are,
essentially, attempts to solve some of the perennial problems.

---

* Bernece Simon is a professor at the School of Social Service Administration,
  University of Chicago, Chicago, Illinois.

Purposes and Goals of Field Instruction

The goals and purposes of field instruction should grow out of and be related to the goals of the curriculum of which it is a part. Field instruction cannot and should not stand above and apart from the curriculum in which it is found. Nevertheless, it is important to be clear about the specific goals of field instruction, in general and in any given curriculum. It is important to identify the "why" of field instruction in college and/or university education because field instruction is enormously expensive, its "academic" quality is always in question and its unique contribution to student learning is easily lost in the murkiness that is stirred up by the managerial problems that derive from it.

A basic, general, descriptive purpose for field instruction is derived from Charlotte Towles' writing:

Professional education is education for use. Therefore, that education should include the opportunity for the student to learn to use knowledge and to experience himself as helper under careful, individualized guidance and helping tutelage. 1/

This statement is not only descriptive of the general purpose of field instruction, but it also has in it the unique contributions of field instruction to student learning. These are: the opportunity for individualization of the student's learning needs and adaptation of teaching to these needs, an opportunity for the student to put knowledge to use in the service of others, and an opportunity for the student to experience himself or herself in the professional role.

A salient feature of this approach to the purposes of field instruction is that it is student-and-learning-centered and that it is related to the practice elements contained in the general objectives for social work education. The level of the learning emphasis in this statement of purpose is of utmost significance. It is cast in general terms and is directed toward the transferability of the knowledge and experiences that are offered in field instruction. These factors convert mere experiences into field instruction and clearly distinguish the latter from apprenticeship, which is learning to give specific services in the specific way of a specific agency.

Recent elaborations in descriptive statements of the purpose of field instruction in the social work curriculum emphasize field instruction as the site for integration of all the content of social work learned in the classroom. This integrative emphasis produces a content focus, as against

---

1/

Charlotte Towle, The Learner in Education for the Professions (Chicago, Illinois: University of Chicago, 1954), pp. 3-23; and "The Place of Help in Supervision," Social Service Review, Vol. 37, No. 4 (December 1963). Also in Helping, ed. Helen Harris Perlman. (Chicago, University of Chicago: 1969), pp. 164-186.

student-learning focus, which has resulted in pushing the field teaching-learning enterprise to higher and higher levels of abstraction, more and more comparable to classroom form and content. This development is probably one aspect of the continuing evolution from agency-bound apprentice-ship to field instruction as a recognized core of the social work education curriculum. Care must be taken, however, that we do not follow the usual social work route of extreme pendulum swings. Field instruction must not become so "academic" that we attenuate or give up that which provides the raison d'etre for it and affords a unique learning for students. It should be noted that the integrative function of field instruction is thoroughly imbedded in the Towle-derived statement of general purpose. But, the other crucial element in that statement is the emphasis placed on the student's development as a professional. This development, which does not stop when formal education is ended, is the essence of integration.

It is possible to summarize the reasons why field instruction is essential to the social work curriculum as follows:

1. The central reason is the one formulated by Towle and others. Since the learning is learning for use, a critical aspect of professional education is the opportunity the student has to experience putting it to use and seeing how it fits together to make the practice of the profession possible.

2. The service professions require that the professional be capable of using himself and his knowledge in the service of the other. Professional education, therefore, should offer this opportunity in circumstances in which there is guidance and help to the student to experience himself as helper, to reflect on and analyze his activity, to develop his ability in this area and to gain gradual understanding of and responsibility for use of himself and his knowledge.

3. In those service professions where students leave school and immediately enter practice, there should be the opportunity beforehand for guided, instructed learning of the processes and methods of practice. This is best done in the field.

These reasons, or the "why" of field instruction, are tied together by the assumption that the use of knowledge in practice, the use of one's self as helper and the development of the beginning ability to carry professional responsibility within the framework of the principles and processes of practice are developed best in an academic situation according to some rational educational plan that is generally applicable to all students. This assumption also serves as a built-in safeguard against apprentice training provided that the field teaching methods support the elements of the assumption.

These educational reasons for field instruction are justification
enough for it. But, in addition, there is interesting support for this
position from the contemporary learning-teaching scene. The support comes
from the hunger young students have for experiential, personal learning--
learning that has specific, unique meaning for the individual student and
learning that derives from gut level response to experience. It is no
accident that students describe their learning experiences in terms of
being "turned on" or "turned off" and identify their goal as "doing their
own thing." Although this approach to learning for professional practice
is highly questionable, it is probable that if field instruction were not
already included in the social work curriculum, we would have to invent it
to meet students' demands for immediate, experiential, existential learning.
Other educational programs which were previously limited to classroom and
book-learning have done this very thing. It is likely that the experience of
hunger of young students is one reason why several medical schools introduce
their first year students to some kind of clinical work instead of waiting
until the third year, as in the traditional medical school curriculum. Law
students organize legal aid clinics even when their law schools do not have
them, not only to feel relevant, but also to experience the practice of law.
Various undergraduate "academic" courses are accompanied by field experiences
to meet the learning preferences of students, to make theory come alive, and
to demonstrate relevance. It is possible that field instruction is an old,
tried idea whose time has come. More important than the apparent vindication
of the idea of field instruction as a course in an academic curriculum is
the fact that in the social work curriculum it has evolved as a disciplined,
goal-directed educational experience, having academic form and content
peculiar to the nature of the experience and its goals. This evolution is
important to keep in mind so that the effort to adapt to apparently new
learning patterns of contemporary students does not lead us into regressive
repetitions of mistakes in our past. The general objectives of field instruction are directed toward discipline of the student's thinking, doing and
feeling in the service of others, not free expression of his own thing in
the sole service of his private self-development. Professional self-development is the end that is sought in professional education.

The appearance of field instruction-like experiences in college courses
and the change in timing of certain aspects of medical and legal education,
along with students' learning preferences call attention to a perennially
unsolved problem in social work education. This is the question of the timing
and form of field instruction in the overall curriculum.

The issue of timing and form is essentially an issue of whether integration of theory and practice is more coherent and useful when theory is
presented before the student undertakes field practice or whether integration
is more truly his when the challenge of learning theory and putting it to use
go together. This educational problem has respectable arguments on both
sides which may be one reason among many that it goes unresolved.

Briefly and too simply these arguments are:

<u>For study of theory before field instruction is undertaken:</u>

1. When students undertake field placements as soon as they enroll
   in social work education, the message that students receive is
   that knowledge, or science, if you will, is essentially denigra-
   ted in this profession but that skill in practice, or artistry,
   is everything. Thus, students immediately become most thoroughly
   engaged in field learning; they neither respect nor tolerate
   classroom work that is not directly connected to their field
   experiences. Besides the critical issue of the depreciation of
   knowledge, the argument adds that under these circumstances field
   instruction cannot be safeguarded against apprentice training.
   (It is an interesting paradox that it seems less and less common
   for students to be solely engaged by field instruction. They
   seem to value <u>good</u> classroom courses for what they are: the
   substance and support of their learning in the field. This is
   paradoxical in relation to their push for individually meaningful
   learning experiences.)

2. In order for the student to undertake professional action in the
   disciplined, analytical and self-aware way that our objectives
   require, it is necessary that he have a coherent base of knowledge
   to guide and direct his action. This base can have coherence only
   when it is presented as a whole without the interference of the
   pressures for action in the field and the temporarily incoherent
   use of theory in response to the exigencies of the "real life"
   situations in the field.

Many social work educators find these arguments convincing. They have
put their convictions to work by developing new patterns for relationship
between class and field learning. In some graduate social work programs,
the students' entry into field instruction is delayed for from five weeks
to a semester. One graduate school has developed a pattern in which students
have only classroom work during the first graduate year and in the second
year they have only field instruction accompanied by a combined methods-
practice seminar. The concern for integration of theory and practice is
also dealt with by the use of various kinds of laboratory methods in the
classroom. Block field placement is another approach to this view, even
though this approach did not originate from the educational dilemma, but
rather from the expedient solution to geographical problems.

<u>For concurrent study of theory and field instruction:</u>

1. Since the aim of professional education is the harmonious and
   simultaneous use of "head, heart and hand," 2/ the most economical

---

2/

This felicitous phrase was originated by C. Towle and used by her in
various discussions and writings on professional education.

way of attaining this objective is to start the student immediately to work on the development of this kind of wholeness of thinking, feeling and doing. This, the proponents say, is accomplished best when the student moves back and forth between formal classroom presentation of theory and its elaboration and application in the realities of the field.

2. The progressive development of field practice as instruction requires that theory and other knowledge be imparted in the field, as well as in the classroom, so that the student has a basis and guide for his action in the field which frequently outruns the range and depth of classroom content. Thus theory is perceived by the student as alive, relevant, and necessary for professional doing. In addition, the reality of professional learning is underscored and its content enhanced and enriched where the student is challenged by the natural "happenings" in the field to search for a cognitive framework by which to understand and to respond to the fortuitous events.

3. The study of theory, as theory, is deepened when the student has the opportunity to consider it at a slight distance (as in the concurrent classroom courses) from the imperatives of human need but simultaneous with his experience of the impact of human need. This permits the development of a truly critical attitude toward the substance of the theory and its application.

Social work educators who espouse these arguments have developed several patterns to aid the process of integration that is implied in their point of view. There is the traditional concurrent class and field pattern in which there is "exploitation" of the opportunities that naturally arise in an agency situation. A new pattern requires careful **parallel** teaching in class and field. That is, when certain aspects of theory are presented in class, the pattern requires that the field settings provide the opportunity for the student to put this aspect to use immediately. Thus, the field placement becomes the laboratory for the classroom. The logical result, however, of the concurrent class and field argument is found in another new pattern that provides for a combined theory-practice seminar, taught in the field in relation to students' field experiences by the faculty field instructor or by a team composed of a classroom teacher or teachers and the field instructor.

These are the time-honored arguments about the timing and form of field instruction in the social work curriculum. It is fair to say that both positions are supportable. Decisions in favor of one or the other are usually made in relation to conviction and expedience. Unfortunately, expedience is usually masked by ex post facto educational rationalizations that do not contribute to the clarification of whatever position is espoused.

It is possible that in social work education at the baccalaureate level this particular pedagogic dilemma will not pose the problems it has in graduate education. The nature of undergraduate education in social work is such that the historical split between theory and practice may not occur. The student who chooses a social work major will enter that course of study with his liberal arts base current and recent. It should be possible for the social work faculty to exploit its location in undergraduate studies in two ways. It may be possible for the social work faculty to participate in the formulation of the liberal arts options. More importantly, the social work instructors should be able to make immediate use of and enhance the liberal arts foundation in the construction and operation of the social work major program. That is, the theory and other knowledge from the liberal arts course of study can be called upon for its implications and applications for social work knowledge and theory. Students can be expected to examine and analyze problems in social work in relation to what they know from the social sciences, humanities, etc. They can be expected to undertake "social criticism" in relation to the actual and proposed solutions to social problems. In addition, the specific contributions of the foundation liberal arts to social work knowledge and theory can be identified at the same time that the unique core of social work is elucidated, perhaps in Bartlett's notion of the gestalt or configuration of knowledge, values, purpose, sanction and method. 3/ Since the nature of undergraduate education is such that it is immediate and concurrent with field practice, with careful thought this can be capitalized on for the objective of integration. For instance, social welfare and social work can be developed in their relation to the eternal human issues of justice, truth, and ethics. The practice of social work (field instruction) is then one expression, among many, of the various efforts to achieve man's ideals.

It has been necessary to include questions of timing and form of field instruction in the discussion of the basic purposes of field instruction because the relationship between purposes, goals, content, and format is complex and has considerable impact on the planning and implementation of field instruction. This interrelationship must be considered in the development of any of its elements.

If field instruction is part of the social work curriculum, then its goals should be derived from the goals of that curriculum and, therefore, should be specific for a specific school. Even though this principle should guide the development of field instruction in any given curriculum, there

---

3/

Harriett Bartlett, Analyzing Social Work Practice by Fields (National Association of Social Workers, New York, 1961), p. 19.

are general statements of the goals of field instruction which can be adapted and elaborated into specific objectives. One such statement is paraphrased from Werner Boehm's view of field instruction: Field instruction is that part of the social work curriculum where the student has the opportunity to bring together all the knowledge from the curriculum to identify and use its relevance to learn social work practice. This goal relates to the social work curriculum; it recognizes that teaching social work practice is the major function of field instruction and it has in it the integrative potential that is the significant, unique value of this part of the curriculum. The integrative potential is played out as the student experiences what it means to be a social worker and has the opportunity through guidance and instruction to see and experience how knowledge is put to use, and most important, why it is necessary. This goal permits the specification of objectives to make learning and integration possible.

There may be, however, reason to question how specific objectives for field instruction in the undergraduate curriculum should be. The freedom that undergraduate social work faculty has from history, tradition and vested interests should permit creative approaches to the development of objectives. In addition, the present fluid state of the social work profession and of social work education requires considerable flexibility and diversity in the development of undergraduate social work curricula. The pressure of the need for flexibility and diversity is seen in the varying and complex objectives set by the four university-agency teams that participated in this project. One example of this pressure is seen in the way that the schools have attempted to serve several equally powerful objectives: liberal arts education, preparation for entry into social work practice, preparation for entry into graduate professional education, to list only the ones most often cited. It seems difficult, if not impossible, to formulate objectives for field instruction that can coherently meet these various objectives. But, neither is it useful, in the current scene, for objectives and content to be too specific. For instance, consider the objective of preparation of the student for beginning entry into the practice of social work. When this objective is chosen, then field instruction ought to be directly related to it. In today's world this is easier said than done because several questions must be answered first including: (1) What is the social work profession; what is the practice of social work? (2) Is it possible to prepare students for the exploding diversity in social work practice today? If so, how? (3) Given these questions, is it possible to identify objectives, plan content and devise methods of field instruction that will hold up over time and diversity?

Field Instruction as Liberal Education

There may be another way to look at these questions as they relate to education for social work in the undergraduate years. This way lies within the liberal education concept. In the Robert Maynard Hutchins tradition,

liberal education is to furnish, hone, and discipline the mind and to
prepare the student for responsible citizenship. This view of education
requires objectives and content that will produce these outcomes, rather
than outcomes of the specificity of preparation for professional practice
as we now think of it. Edward Levi, president of the University of Chicago,
has advanced the idea that many professions which require graduate education
may not have the range or depth of content or require the time implied by
graduate education. He includes his own profession, law, in this conjecture. 4/
But, in including law, he suggests that the study of law provides a liberal
education. In this interpretation of liberal education, social welfare,
like the law, could be considered to be a study of the "liberal arts."
That is, it is study that requires the examination, analysis, comparison
and synthesis of ideas brought to bear on social welfare problems and study
that identified the relationship of specific problems such as poverty,
racism, and mental health to more general problems of mankind such as
justice, truth, and ethics. Social work, in this approach, becomes a specific example of the use of social welfare ideas (from wherever derived) for
the solution of specific aspects of mankind's general problems. Thus, if
the liberal education objective of undergraduate education is the most
significant objective of an undergraduate social work curriculum, then the
objectives and content of field instruction must be closely tied to the
liberal education ideal. How would field instruction fit into this framework for social work education? And, how could objectives and content for
it deal with the questions about preparing students in a way that would
hold up over time and diversity? If field instruction were treated as part
of a liberal oriented curriculum, it might look something like this.

The social work curriculum would be cast in a framework of the basic
goals and values related to solutions of society's and mankind's problems.
These goals and values would undergird all social work practice, however
defined and specified. Content and methods of teaching would be directed
toward continuous honing and disciplining of the mind, toward the development of the student's capacity for analysis and synthesis. Content and
method would aim to teach the student to think, to give him a way of thinking
about social welfare and social work problems and solutions. The central
objective of field instruction, then, would be an emphasis on the student's
use of a way of thinking of knowledge and of himself as enabler, helper,
advocate--whatever roles are identified as central to social work practice.
These objectives and the content necessary for their implementation would
hold regardless of the agency selected for field instruction or the social
work methods used in the field setting.

4/

Edward H. Levi. Address delivered during annual meeting of American Law
Institute, Washington, D.C., May 23, 1969; address delivered during
Annual Meeting of Association for General and Liberal Studies, October
29, 1970. (Mimeographed.)

The universal and pervasive problem of the relationship of the individual to society may serve as one example of how appropriate content might be identified for this non-technical approach to learning social work practice.

It could be said that the fundamental issues for individuals today are: the impact of anomie, including ambiguity of interpersonal relationships; that is, questions of trust, meaningfulness, authenticity, and communication; problems in self-realization or questions of the boundaries of freedom to be one's self; and problems of the individual's responsibility to society and society's to the individual. Objectives, content, and methods of class and field teaching would be organized around the social work application of relevant knowledge to deal with these kinds of problems no matter how they are expressed. The issue of anomie, for instance, might be approached, at one level, by examining and analyzing a community and the resources it allocates toward helping individuals develop human ties, and extend participation beyond their own lives, as well as toward demonstrating the community's concern for the individuals in it. The universal issue of relationship ambiguity might serve as the framework to study human growth and development theories, principles of professional relationship, ways in which problems of trust, communication and meaning are expressed, and ways by which they can be ameliorated. The universality of the issue would be the context in which the student could experience himself as a helper and develop his capacity to function in a professional role. Similarly, it is possible to consider the other issues for individuals as the organizing principles around which other content can be developed.

These ideas are offered as a way of implementing liberal education objectives for social work education at the baccalaureate level. But, they have some concrete advantages for curriculum building in the shifting sands of higher education and of the profession of social work. This approach seems to allow for the flexible but rational adaptation of content to the demands of diversity and rapid change in the profession. Content can be open-ended when the objectives are stable and directed toward the development of the student as thinker and disciplined doer. The goal of transferability, of the ways to use knowledge and self seems more attainable in this context, as does the goal of integration of theory with practice. The liberal education context also provides freedom for creative invention of the conceptual scheme for undergraduate social work education that is related to the goals and aspirations of the college or university of which the program is a part and to the general social welfare issues that may vary from region to region. This approach enables a wide variety of field instruction content and patterns to meet the same objectives. Finally, the breadth of this framework for social work education dictates that field instruction content be organized as configurations for learning, not tasks to be mastered, and that students be educated for social work practice rather than "trained" to fill slots in one establishment or another.

Two units which participated in this project have the seeds of this approach either in the statements of their objectives or in the elaboration of the content and pattern of field instruction. In one of these programs there is the general objective of preparation of the student for entry into practice, but one of the specific objectives for field instruction is that the student experience or "find himself" as a helper in a service delivery system. The expected outcome of this program is the emergence of the student's self-understanding, self-discipline, and development of confidence in his ability to be of service to others. In this view of field instruction for practice there is a broad conception of employability of the graduate so that specific, ephemeral practice need **not be a consideration** in the choice of content. There is no concrete content structure since content is derived from the creative work field instructor and student do together to **enable** the student to "find himself" as a helper in a service system. There are potential difficulties with this plan. One **crucial** one is how real, everyday connections are made between the objectives, content, and methods of the field instruction courses. Another possible issue in this plan is that it may be so process- and student-self-development-oriented that content (knowledge) which is the basis for process and use of self is, at best, separated from process or, at most lost altogether. But, the important idea in this plan is the objective of educating a person who understands and can manage some of the personal requirements for offering service to others.

The other unit **identifies** the development of the student's ability for "social criticism" as a by-product or sub-objective of its undergraduate social work curriculum. If this were a major objective, it would have a direct and clarifying impact on the objectives and content of field instruction and **would** shape the outcomes of education in specified, concrete but transferable ways. But, the significant aspect of this "throw-away" objective is that it, too, is a tentative step toward a liberal education context for a social work major course of study.

The importance of the relationship between objectives and content for field instruction has been belabored here because of the conviction that there must be clarity about objectives to begin to achieve clarity and co-herence in content even though there is no guarantee that one will produce the other. The idea of liberal education objectives and content for under-graduate social work education has been emphasized because it seems to promise a way to prevent the development of new problems or recurrence of old problems in social work education, such as the "training" of technicians, the use of the educational institution for apprenticeship or special interest purposes and the dilution, even degradation, of the purposes of "higher" education. The liberal education concept might, in its implementation, make a contribution to the further and different development of social work knowledge and practice theory. Finally, clarity about objectives for field instruction and the broadening of the context in which it is developed should

serve as a liberating force in the development of methods of field instruction that will fit objectives and content. The central issue in education
is objectives and content and all else is, at this time in history, a matter
of debatable opinion.

Form and Patterns of Field Teaching

One of the most frequent cliches of social work education criticism is
that while considerable evolutionary change has taken place in most of the
curriculum form and content, there has been little or no change in field
instruction. This observation is justified if the focus of critical examination is on the form and patterns of field instruction. It is a less
accurate statement if the criticism encompasses examination of content,
internal methods of teaching in the field, and expectations of students 5/
and field settings. The evolutionary changes in field instruction were related to the gradual diminution of the apprenticeship aspects as these were
reflected in content that was derived from the specific practice of any given
field setting. There was a clear movement from teaching the specific practice
of the agency to organization of content that was derived from the basic structure and principles of practice being taught with the goal that field learning
should be at a level of generalization that would allow for transfer of knowledge
and skill to practice in any setting. Those were the articulated aims of most
schools of social work. That there was often a gap between aims and implementation attests only to the fact that field instruction is a human endeavor.
There was also progressive movement in teaching methods and attitudes toward
field instruction among field instructors and agencies. The changes in attitudes were twofold: (a) for agencies, there was increasing recognition that
students were placed in agencies to learn practice, not to assist the agency
in meeting its service commitments and pressures and (b) for field instructors,
there was a deepening understanding and acceptance of the role of teacher as
contrasted to the role of therapist. 6/ This was true no matter what the social

---

5/

See, for instance, A Standard for Measuring the Minimum Acceptable Level of
Performance in First-Year Field Work in Social Casework: Levels Committee
Report. Prepared by Aleanor Merrifield, Jan Linfield, Edythe Jastram.
Pamphlet, School of Social Science Administration, University of Chicago,
1965. A Standard for Measuring the Minimum Acceptable Level of Performance
in Second-Year Field Work in Social Work: Levels Committee Report. Ed.
Aleanor Merrifield and Sylvia Astro. Pamphlet--SSA, University of Chicago,
1964. Final Report Field Instruction Research Project, Wm. E. Gordon,
Margaret L. Schutz, Co-Directors--George Warren Brown School of Social Work,
Washington University, St. Louis, Mo., 1968, pp. 86-108. Mildred Sikkema,
Jeanette Regensberg and Bess Dana, Field Instruction in Graduate Social Work
Education: Old Problems and New Proposals, Council on Social Work Education,
1966, pp. 50-52. Current Patterns in Field Instruction in Graduate Social
Work Education, Ed. Betty Lacy Jones (Council on Social Work Education:
New York, 1969), pp. 125-135.

6/

C. Towle, The Learner, pp. 134-175.

work method being taught, although each introduction into the curriculum of additional social work methods required that the service-apprenticeship role of the student and "therapy" role of the field instructor be worked on de nouveau. It is to be hoped that this phylogenetic compulsion will not be a part of the development of undergraduate social work education. These changes in attitude toward field instruction led to differential uses of the tutorial method, requirements for and uses of student recording, and a tentative movement toward the didactic presentation of content in the field, or group teaching. Most, if not all, of these changes were not clearly or extensively documented by studies or by literature. They may have been too subtle, too uneven or too gradual to have been identified as truly evolutionary even though they were basically revolutionary.

Drastic change in field instruction patterns, forms, and methods was the first order of business when criticism of social work education was at its height. Many changes in field instruction were announced. By and large these were changes in form rather than in objectives and content. Over time, however, the innovations in patterns of field instruction became connected with changes in content and specification of objectives. Three categories of changes seem important for consideration here because they demonstrate the necessary relationship between objectives, content and teaching forms and methods and because they continue to be refined while generating further debate. These are: the varied uses of agencies as field placements; the increasing use of didactic teaching in the field, or group teaching; and the use of full-time field instructors, either agency-based or university-based.

Use of agency field placements

Over the last twenty-five to thirty years, students have been placed in a different agency in each of the two years of graduate education. The first placement usually was used to introduce the student to the generic core or basic structure of the social work practice method he had chosen and to start his development as a professional social worker. The second placement was used for the student to apply and elaborate this base in a specific field of practice.

The variations in agency use that have recently been introduced have been directed toward the goal of making it realistically possible for field instruction to be the site where the student puts together and applies knowledge gleaned from all parts of the curriculum--that is, to enhance integration of knowledge and practice. Elaborations of this goal have included the aims of engaging the student to learn social work practice, to break through what was perceived as a narrow, technical orientation to practice and to support certain changes in the organization of content in classroom courses.

These goals have been implemented by the development of the concept of the teaching-learning center which has taken many forms. In the most rudimentary state, this concept is played out by the assignment of the student to one agency and one field instructor with pre-arrangement for him to have experiences in other agencies to fill in gaps in social work practice of the base agency, to give him the opportunity to put classroom knowledge to use when this is not possible in the base agency and to offer him the opportunity to be involved, at one level or another, in the spectrum of social work responses to social welfare problems. For example, the student may have his base assignment in a family agency and supplementary experiences in a neighborhood house, a grass roots organization, etc. This pattern of field instruction is frequently embarked upon as support for a multi-methods curriculum, especially in the first year. There are, in this pattern, various potential problems. For the school and agencies there are administrative problems that need constant negotiation. The field instructor responsibility for monitoring and evaluating the student's experiences and learning is complicated and frequently difficult. Educationally, this pattern re-opens the question of the balance between depth and breadth in the student's learning and it presents a fairly large integrative task for the student.

Another form of the teaching-learning center is similar to the first, but is more rationally planned. The student is assigned to a specific cluster of agencies and to one field instructor. Learning opportunities are organized within the cluster in some kind of parallel concurrence with classroom content and in relation to the concept of progression. In this form, the field is laboratory for the classroom. Other organizing ideas for the use of the cluster are support of a multi-methods curriculum, and/or a social problem concentration, for example, delinquency, mental retardation, poverty, etc. The major difference in this use is that the cluster is used according to some organizing principles and the administrative problems are minimized by agreements by the agencies to be used in this way and to plan with the school ways in which this form of field instruction can be facilitated. The heavy burden for the field instructor and the integrative task for the student seem to be similar to the first pattern. In many instances, the administrative burden for the field instructor is relieved by the use of preceptors in the various cluster agencies. They are usually agency-employed social workers. Teaching and evaluation functions are left for the assigned field instructor. The preceptor helps the student with the administrative aspects of the agency, guides him through the details of service management, and may carry some of the service responsibility. This seems to be a productive division of functions and responsibilities, provided that division can be clarified and maintained with relative stability.

The most sophisticated form of the teaching-learning center is either the social welfare center that is devised by the school of social work, as a new multi-service agency, or a consortium of agencies that is established with agreements tnat the agencies will give priority to teaching and research. These centers are analogous to teaching hospitals for medical schools. In these situations, the administrative and teaching problems noted above are minimized even though there may be others indigenous to the school being responsible, at some level, for a service agency.

All three forms usually, but not always, have faculty-based full-time field instructors who have large units of students. In addition, the specific student-field instructor work in the center is supported by a field practice seminar manned either by selected classroom faculty or teams of classroom and field faculty. The focus of these seminars is to identify the generalizations that can be drawn from the diverse experiences students have in the field and to connect these back to the students' classroom work. This pattern for field instruction evolved in relation to the objectives cited but there was an additional motivation for its development. This pattern insures that schools of social work, having the responsibility for the students' education, also have the power and resources to control the content, form and method of this crucial aspect of education.

Still another pattern that has recently emerged is the assignment of students to the same agency and field instructor for the full two years. In this pattern, the field instructor is also the practice method classroom teacher. This pattern evolved to support a generalist social work practice. In the generalist concept, the method of intervention flows from the nature of the person-problem-situation configuration. This means that field agencies must expand their view of their functions, if not actually expand their functions. Students become involved in various forms of out-reach, advocacy and institutional and policy change requiring extensive and intensive collaboration and continuous negotiation of sanction for their intervention plans and activities. All of this takes time--time for relationships and plans to evolve and time for students to see where the process is going and how it will turn out. Thus, to enable progression in learning, planning, and accomplishment for the student, it seemed imperative for the student to stay in the same placement for two years. Various methods are used to introduce teacher and content diversity into this pattern which otherwise can feel rigid to the student. In this pattern, too, the field instructor carries a heavy administrative and substantive burden and the student has a very heavy integrative challenge which is frequently a burden.

The opposite pattern has **already** been noted. That is the one in which the first year of graduate work is entirely in the classroom and the second year full-time field instruction supported by a methods-practice seminar.

All these innovative patterns are attempts at solution of various professional education problems. Most of them had been tried in one form or another at some time in the history of social work education. They are innovative, however, in that old ideas were cast into new configurations, with objectives directed toward a higher level preparation and with content chosen and organized in relation to the contemporary scene. All of these patterns and forms of field instruction are enormously complicated, frequently messy, and often more honored in the breach than in the doing. And, there is, as yet, no certainty that these forms and patterns produce better delivery of content, enhance integration or develop a better base for practice. But they are efforts related to a concept of social work function and social work practice which have shaped curriculum objectives and content.

Group Teaching in the Field

This development has taken many forms which will not be detailed here. The field practice seminars noted above is one form. The most common form uses group teaching as the major vehicle for the delivery of content in the field with tutorial or individual conferences used on an as-needed, supplemental basis. The form is less important than the rationale for this approach to teaching in the field.

Since the content for the teaching of the group is derived from the students' field assignments, the substance and process in this teaching provide a model for and experience in the conceptualization of practice. The examination, analysis and criticism of the students' practice culminate in the extraction of principles and generalizations which can be related to theory and knowledge derived from many parts of the curriculum. In addition, students' learning needs, collective and individual, are identified in this process. The content is enriched because each student learns not only from his assignment but also from the assignments of all the other students. When teaching is undertaken in this way there is greater possibility of equality of learning opportunity for all students in the unit since they are exposed to the same content at the same time in the same climate. At the same time, variations in individual learning can be dealt with either in the group or in individual conferences. The possibility of peer learning is clearly a major factor in this kind of teaching. Peer exchange and working together is known to enhance learning but, in addition, it is an important source of learning for adults and it encourages and enhances appropriate learning and performance autonomy and interdependence. Finally, there is dilution of the traditionally intense field instructor-student relationship and dependence which has been thought to constrict creative development of students' abilities. There is the important fact that group teaching in the field reduces the enormous cost of field instruction because it is obvious that one field instructor can teach and be responsible for more students. Many field instructors who use this method of field instruction attest to the fact that they can comfortably manage a unit of ten students and be confident that the students are learning well.

Experience with group teaching seems to indicate that the rationale for its use is appropriate. But, experience has also shown that flexibility in its use is necessary to allow for differential decisions as to timing, length, content, and need for group teaching-learning sessions and individual tutorial sessions. That is, care has to be exercised that the major value of field instruction--individualization of students' learning needs and patterns--is not lost in the push for more efficiency in teaching and the thrust for higher levels of learning.

In fact, this care must be exercised in relation to the various innovations in patterns of field teaching. There is no doubt that method and format flexibility and experimentation are needed in field teaching in order to develop content creatively and meet objectives. The various experiments should be examined not only for how they support and enhance objectives and content but also for how the unique aspects of field instruction are supported and enhanced. The uniqueness of field instruction in the social work learning enterprise that must be supported and enhanced is the opportunity for individualization of student learning needs against stable expectations, the development of student as helper and the opportunity for him to use his knowledge and himself in real life social work practice situations. The movement, implicit in the various changes in field instruction, to shape it to be more and more like the classroom should be carefully monitored against the possibility that the challenge, freedom and potential creativity inherent in the opportunistic quality of teaching and learning are not dammed by rigid requirements of form and constricting logical coherence with the rest of the curriculum.

Summary

This discussion has attempted to make and to elaborate the simple idea that purposes and objectives of undergraduate field instruction should be derived from the purposes and objectives of the social work curriculum and that these should dictate the content and methods of teaching in the field. The other major idea in the presentation is the possibility that some of the problems of field instruction in the undergraduate social work curriculum might be solved if field instruction courses were planned within a liberal education context. It was also suggested that a liberal education view of field instruction might prevent the repetition, in undergraduate social work education, of some of the more perennial problems in graduate social work education.

THE IMPACT OF UNDERGRADUATE FIELD INSTRUCTION
PROGRAMS ON MANPOWER DEVELOPMENT

by

William G. Hill*

Field instruction is a costly form of education for the university, the learner, as well as for the agency which provides staff and facilities. None of the partners in the educational process gain if there is an attempt to provide "cheap" education. A more accurate assessment of both the costs and benefits of field instruction programs, especially under-graduate field instruction programs, is desirable. Using a cost-benefit analysis, we need to ask realistically what are the costs and what are the benefits of this program to an agency. 1/

Agencies throughout the nation are being confronted with enormous demands for services by the users of these services. This has required re-examining the availability of manpower in relation to delivery of services. It has also brought forth the need to examine activities carried out within administrative units of service to determine whether an individual worker with certain identifiable skills can or cannot adequately provide specific services. There has been in the history of social work heavy reliance upon the MSW trained person to carry out this responsibility. In addition, there has been heavy use of individuals possessing a baccalaureate degree. In the past these individuals have received for the most part on-the-job training in a specific agency setting where they generally served as apprentices to the MSW trained staff.

As a result of this phenomenon, considerable confusion has developed with respect to what standards should be applied, what kinds of services can be offered by people with less than an MSW and what kinds of educational experiences better prepare undergraduate students to function effectively in

---

* William G. Hill is Director of the Office of Specialized Agency Services, Family Service Association of America, New York, New York.

1/
   "Schedule for Presentations and Discussions" distributed to the participants of the Undergraduate Field Experience Demonstration Project Evaluation Workshop held in New Orleans, Louisiana, April 28-30, 1971 (mimeographed, pp. 3-4).

a social work setting. Effective utilization presupposes the existence of a national policy within a profession providing for a deliberate allocation of resources through means that are intended to achieve a chosen end. Such a policy also assumes "the existence of resources--men, organization, money, time, ideas--and suggests ways of bringing them to bear. Finally, it implies that there is agreement and collaboration among men and institutions to execute the steps of the policy." 2/

AN OPERATIONAL DEFINITION

Manpower Development

In the Unabridged Edition of The Random House Dictionary of the English Language, several definitions are given for manpower ranging from "the power supplied by the physical exertions of a man or men" to "power in terms of men available or required: the manpower of an army."

Neither does the dictionary help in defining the word, "power," for which it offers some twenty-six definitions. The first or primary definition was "ability to do or act; capability of doing or accomplishing something." The second definition stated, "usually, powers, particular faculties or capabilities of body or mind; creative powers; the power of speed." Synonyms for power include the notions of capacity, energy and strength.

The National Association of Social Workers', for example, suggests that it is composed of at least nine elements: education, career development, employment, differential utilization, personnel practices, legislation, and competence.

We must therefore conclude that the term, "manpower development," is somehow related to participation by people in work activities, activities that are organized in some kind of fashion that makes it possible for one to understand and analyze a particular work system with respect to determining its purposes and goals.

Cost-Benefit

A recent study entitled, The Cost and Output of Graduate Social Work Education: An Exploratory Study, noted that there is no satisfactory definition for the concept of "cost." 3/ This is true in general accountancy, and more

---

2/
Henry W. Riecken, "The Federal Government and Social Science Policy," The Annals of the American Academy of Political and Social Science, 394 (March 1971), p. 101.

3/
The Cost and Output of Graduate Social Work Education: An Exploratory Study (Cooper and Company, Stamford, Connecticut), U.S. Department of Health, Education, and Welfare, Social and Rehabilitation Service (Contract SRS 69-11). U.S. Government Printing Office, Washington, D.C., (1970).

specifically in social work education. One way of looking at cost-benefits emphasizes an "exchange concept" (quid pro quo) or "something for something." The transactions which accountants deal with are based on "factual" accounts, on specific expenditures for specific goods. For certain purposes, this way of looking at the world is quite fitting and proper. However, it is my conviction that there is a major weakness with the accountant design especially as it applies to social work education. This is related to the problem of planning for change. Accounting data deals with past performances not with future performances. I am very much aware of this difficulty in my own responsibilities for long-range planning where there is a natural tendency to seek out the controller or financial officer to take the major responsibility for future planning. It is a pitfall to be avoided since planning requires assessment of future directions, not just a rendering of past performance records. I might also venture the notion that such a concept has a rather simplistic frame of reference. It has what I would call a tubular or stimulus-response characteristic which would work very well within a closed system where processes are reversible. It would not work in an open system where processes are never static.

This study also emphasized the difficulties that economics theory had in handling the concept of cost. This was due to costs being defined in a number of different ways--from the aggregate of physical factors of production to total (market) price of the factors or inputs. To quote from the report: "Historically, the economist's concern with cost has been largely descriptive rather than normative. In other words, he has tried to describe why the economic aspects of our society are what they are .... He has been concerned very little with the determination of what these units ought to do, and has usually assumed that, sooner or later, these units (firms and individuals) will find out, and do, what is good for them, that is, they will act in their own best interest. There was no need, for example, to educate these units on the nature of costs." 4/

In order to apply the problem of cost-benefit to social work education, the researchers opted for what they called, "a decision-theoretic approach." In pursuing this approach, they recognized that oftentimes what may be viewed as a cost by one might well be a benefit to someone else. For example, if one student is required to study X number of hours more than another, are the additional hours a cost or a benefit? 5/

The authors of this research report stress that one cannot tell, "a cost from a benefit without a program." 6/ Without a program, cost-benefit notions become mental exercises.

4/

Ibid., p. 19.

5/

Ibid., p. 21.

6/

Loc. cit.

The matter of whether a program should be undertaken, supported, and continued requires that one have information. This information should be both generalized and specific. For example, in Family Service Association of America, we speak of our organization having two purposes, namely, rendering direct services to member family service agencies and acting as a collective representative for the agencies in matters affecting family life. These two statements are useful, but when it comes to a decision about whether to undertake a new program or not, it doesn't help very much. What is required is more specificity, more information about whether one particular course of action is better than another. In this sense, the above mentioned report emphasized the essentiality of decision-making in cost-benefit analysis and how outcomes or consequences involve choices or preferences. With respect to the Undergraduate Field Experience Demonstration Project, it is necessary to know whether its purpose was to produce better qualified persons for provision of direct services to clients or to develop a systematic body of knowledge for curricula building purposes? Was its purpose to demonstrate that meaningful transactions can occur between two systems when formalized arrangements have been established? With respect to the Project's impact on manpower development, has the cost been too high if graduates of social work programs find no more opportunity for social work employment than graduates with other majors.

PROBLEMS OF EMPLOYING AGENCIES

The need to rely upon an outmoded apprenticeship educational program for individuals with less than an MSW is well-known to most social welfare agencies in this country. Presumably employing agencies will prefer to hire individuals who have received an indentifiable formal social work educational experience at the undergraduate level.

One of the greatest burdens faced by social agencies today is sorting out educational experiences of persons who are being considered for employment. At the present time much of the activity engaged by agencies wishing to employ individuals with less than an MSW is a hit or miss affair. Because no standardized frame of reference is available to prospective employers, they must rely upon instinct, intuition, and the like. They have to place heavy value on an individual's maturity and personality in the absence of a documented formalized educational experience. It would thus appear that one of the greatest benefits coming out of this project is that of setting in motion a systematic approach to social work education at the undergraduate level. An additional problem facing employers of baccalaureate level social workers is that of "differential utilization"; how can one most effectively identify those tasks which are best done by MSW workers and another level which is best performed by BA workers? Differential utilization of personnel is self-evident and required a framework or configurational pattern for personnel deployment. Such an ordered approach would make it possible to employ individuals within a system of recognizable rewards and task accomplishment expectations.

In this connection, simple, routine tasks usually are assigned to the baccalaureate level social workers. How these individuals fit into an overall continuum of service to people is not evident. It is as if individuals in this "classification" scheme become blocked off from those with professional graduate social work education. This results in a climate of isolation, disappointment, and frustration for both groups of workers. Ideas and hopes for advancement "within the ranks" to new responsibilities and additional job satisfactions are not realized. In effect, the BA worker becomes locked into a situation where upward movement is not possible.

An example of this state of affairs was recently presented to this writer in a group discussion with some twenty-five social work assistants who came together from a variety of agencies on the East Coast. The remark was made that becoming a social work assistant meant only one thing; that is, the social work assistant could now move from one ghetto to another ghetto but never out of the ghetto. The jobs they had were circumscribed, limited, and not connected with other parts of the social work delivery system.

The need for the development of a meaningful system of manpower differentiation and utilization of social work personnel is evident. The absence of differential utilization plans and clear dilineations of what is expected of those entering social work employment at various levels is burdensome not only to employers, it also makes the task of the social work educator all but impossible. In effect, social work educators are asked to educate students for responsible job entry without being told what it is that the beginning worker will be expected to know or do. Since at this time neither the professional organization nor the employing agencies have provided leadership in resolving this dilemma, social work education has had to face this problem almost alone. We say "almost alone" because important help has come from a number of quarters. The funding by the Veterans Administration of this project (and a companion project to be discussed below) is an important step toward resolving this problem. Beginning efforts are present as evidenced not only by the experience of those who participated in the Undergraduate Field Experience Demonstration Project but also by the findings of another undergraduate social work curriculum building project-- this one sponsored by the Syracuse University School of Social Work and again funded by the Veterans Administration. In this project, a model was proposed for educating the undergraduate for professional social work roles. The Syracuse group proposed a set of expectations for the baccalaureate level social worker that would be applicable to numerous social work settings.

These expectations are as follows:

1. He is able to recognize and work within the purpose and structure of an agency on the goals and constraints of a particular setting and will hold himself accountable for completion of particular assignments within his own competence.

Attendant to the above conclusion by Zimbalist and Anderson is an added thought posed by this writer. Is it possible that within many agencies throughout this country there are positions filled by holders of the MSW which could be adequately filled by those with a B.A. degree in social work? Is it possible that because of a set of circumstances, holders of the MSW have "tailored" their jobs in such routine fashion that an in-depth job analysis would reveal these individuals performing daily low-level tasks? The apparent slowness by which the more tradition-al social service agencies have moved in diversifying their staffing patterns legitimately raises such a question. It is interesting to note that historically social workers with less than an MSW have been employed almost exclusively in the public welfare sector. Also, it is interesting that the emergence of programs generated by the "War on Poverty" have had close associations with public welfare.

There is in this writer's opinion, however, definite rays of hope that individuals with either an A.A. or B.A. degree in social work will be more fully integrated into the whole social welfare system--family service, child welfare, medical, psychiatric. This conclusion is based on several observable trends. One of these is the close association being developed between the voluntary sector and the public sector in social welfare matters. These associations have taken the shape of formal contracts for provision of certain services by voluntary agencies through the utilization of public monies. Such contractual agreements, or purchase of service contracts, usually require the voluntary agencies to employ additional personnel. The contracts also by virtue of being "stated understandings" necessitate des-criptions of what services will be provided, who will provide them, and who will receive them.

As a result of these conditions, agencies who wish to participate in the purchase of service agreements must develop plans which reflect the differential utilization of personnel. Since these plans become contractual agreements, costs must be addressed. This has a way of forcing the agency to examine how it can provide the services at an acceptable price to the buyer. Differential utilization of personnel as reflected in salary data developed by the potential provider of services then facilitates the use of a variety of personnel with particular skills and competency.

An example of the implications of this new phenomenon is seen in family service agencies who have membership in the Family Service Association of America. There has been a steady increase in the employment of individuals with less than the MSW degree. This has not been the result of employing fewer MSW workers but has resulted from an expansion in number and kinds of purchase of service contracts between the family service agencies and public agencies. 10/

10/
    William G. Hill, "Voluntary and Governmental Financial Transactions,"
    Social Casework, Volume 52, Number 6 (June 1971), pp. 356-361.

The point stressed here is that the matter of intensively and extensively examining the types of personnel required to provide the services cannot be avoided because of new services being generated by these agencies through purchase of service contract agreements. This has resulted in the employment of many individuals with less than the MSW degree.

Another example of recent changes in delivery service systems outside the public welfare sector has occurred in the health field. The Joint Commission on the Accreditation of Hospitals, the national standard setting body for some six thousand hospitals, required as of July 1, 1971, that all member hospitals have social services available to patients. The provision of these services must be under the supervision of a qualified professional social worker (MSW or equivalent). Direct service activities can be given by those with less than an MSW. It is likely this new requirement will result in an increase in the number of social workers employed in medical social work settings. It would appear further that undergraduate students who have had the benefit of an educationally focused field instruction program of the kind developed by this project would be well suited as prospective employees.

If one were to relate the above noted events to the developments occuring in undergraduate social work education particularly with regard to field instruction programs, then the recognition of the baccalaureate degree as the first practice degree takes on significance.

COST-BENEFIT OF FIELD INSTRUCTION TO THE AGENCY

Attention to this subject has until recently been mostly confined to field instruction on the graduate level. Irrespective of whether one is talking about graduate or undergraduate social work programs, time spent by employees of an agency in the educational experiences of students represents an expenditure for the agency. The allocation of other agency resources for students, such as physical space, writing materials, and secretarial support represent additional expenditures of scarce resources. At times, the benefits derived from students have been calculated on the basis of the number of clients assisted by the students.

An example of one approach reflecting this way of addressing the subject is a time and cost document prepared by the Family Service Association of America. Participation by professional staff in the education of social work students is identified in two major or discrete ways. The first is time spent in supervision. "This includes time spent supervising individual students in placement; group meetings of students for the purpose of orientation or group discussion of the training experience; field trips, etc. Also includes reading student records, time spent in discussing a student's research project activity;

and written evaluation of student performance prepared for schools." 11/
The second major area of activity identified in this document is that of
staff's work relationships to the school of social work. It, "includes
conferences, either in-person or by telephone or correspondence with a
school representative about a specific student or the student program in
the agency; meetings of agency supervisors called by the school to discuss
various aspects of the student training program." 12/

By combining these two variables (total time spent in student training)
and allocating the time expenditure directly to salaries of workers, a cost
figure was obtained. (It should be noted that most agencies which utilize
such procedures include in their salary data the "indirect costs" or "over-
head expenses" for the workers. These "indirect costs" include actual
space utilized, lights, heat, water, etc.)

It is interesting that in utilizing such an approach for obtaining
cost-benefit information, a survey of member family service agencies in
Family Service Association of America for the years of 1963 through 1969
indicated that the median unit cost per graduate social work student was two
dollars and sixty cents an hour, for each hour the student was in the agency.

This finding tended to support the feeling of the participants in the
workshop that the actual expense to an agency for student training is a
relatively inexpensive matter. (In fact, one might conclude that "it's a
good deal" for the agency.) However, this type of interpretation implies
looking at students as a source of "cheap labor" and that by emphasizing
the dollar value, one de-emphasizes or negates the value of education. The
goal of field instruction is that of students learning, not of providing
services to clients.

Nevertheless, there are benefits accruing to the agency. The presence
of students can "upgrade" the staff of the agency. Their presence can stimulate other staff. It can bring the agency and the university closer together.
The students often are "the ties that bind" the two together. This results
in more awareness of the other and a deeper respect of the problems each is
having. With regard to this latter benefit, it is interesting to note that
a perusal of the four curriculum guides developed out of the project emphasizes
this point. Phrases like "the necessity to integrate" the efforts of both
agency and university, the requirement for "cooperative arrangements," and

---

11/

  Time and Cost Analysis Series (Volume II). Prepared by Department of
  Systems and Statistics, Family Service Association of America, New York
  (December 1968), p. 34.

12/

  Guidelines for the Assessment of Professional Practice in Social Work.
  Prepared by Committee on the Study of Competence, (New York: National
  Association of Social Workers, 1968), p. iv.

the "mutually shared responsibilities" were expressed in these materials reinforcing this position.

With respect to developing harmonious relationships between school and agency, it is evident that the Undergraduate Field Experience Demonstration Project was an effective vehicle. 13/ Such functional relationships are very much needed throughout the system of social work education as emphasized further by the findings of the special committee set up by CSWE to study the length of graduate social work education at the MSW level.

In summary it can be said that the absence of a functional system of manpower utilization, the lack of clarity within the existing disordered system concerning identifiable levels of competence for practice, and the absence of explicit avenues to connect-up in a meaningful manner with other institutions for the purpose of sharing what had been gained in recent years are factors impinging upon a more fruitful cost-benefit of field instruction to the agency.

CONCLUSION

Educational facilities and social agencies must join hands to work toward more meaningful ways to enhance the educational opportunities of students, to assist agencies in working on differential utilization patterns of personnel, and to keep open the possibility for establishing functional career opportunities for individuals with various educational training. Likewise, expansion of job opportunities for persons interested in social welfare as a career is closely associated with the formulation of educational experiences. Contained in this notion is an awareness that the recruitment, selection, training, utilization, and retention of personnel below the master's of social work level has been subject to a wide variety of circumstances. As a result, information very much needed to develop a systematic and rational approach to the use of persons below the MSW level has been sparse, probably inaccurate, and not subject to tests of validity.

It does appear, that in spite of the present recession, new and innovative programs of service delivery have emerged in this nation. Early examination of these new programs in the health and family service fields indicates that considerable attention is being given to the utilization of social work personnel with varying levels of educational training. What is now required is a joining together of all national agencies, public and private, who have "direct service" responsibilities to more seriously explore the impact that undergraduate field instruction programs are making on manpower development so as to benefit from this in a more productive way and consequently become more effective in the delivery of services.

13/

For example, agency staff participation in developing educationally focused field instruction programs--more specifically, curriculum guides--would appear to have great merit as one way of maintaining an open system of exchange between the two as effectively demonstrated by this project.